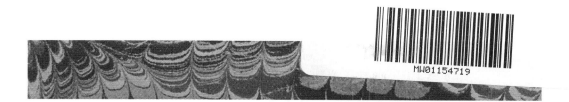

Market Segmentation
An Introduction and Review

Dr. Steven M. Struhl

Principal
Converge Analytic LLC

Marketing
Research
Technique
S E R I E S

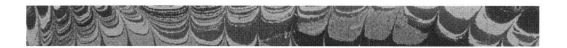

Market Segmentation

Acknowledgements

The author's wife Kathryn, who passed away in 2003, was instrumental in completing the first printing. Her great patience during the many late nights and weekends involved in this book's preparation and her outstanding proof-reading skills were indispensible. Damon Ragusa helped immensely in preparing the original exhibits for the first version of this manuscript, when these were amazingly difficult to do. Again, heartfelt thanks go to both of them.

Some portions of this book represent a revision and updating of material by William D. Neal and a manual on market segmentation developed under contract for SDR, Inc. by Dr. Wilbur Stanton. The author gratefully acknowledges the contributions of these two writers. Where Mr. Neal's materials, some unpublished, are a source, this is noted in the text.

Special discounts are available for larger quantity printings, especially for those purchasing 10,000 copies or more. Special editions, including personalized covers or covers bearing the portrait of the individual requesting the edition or that of a renowned person (Calvin Coolidge and Herbert Hoover have been perennial favorites) can be created for print runs of over 100,000. Send all inquiries to info@convergeanalytic.com.

9 8 7 6 5

Library of Congress Cataloging in Publication Data information is available.
ISBN-13: 978-1492781745
ISBN-10: 1492781746

CONTENTS

Figures

Part 1: Basics, Terms and Getting Through the Jargon

I. Introduction to segmentation

A. Overview

B. A Brief History

C. A Landmark Article

D. Segmentation Basics

E. Principal Questions in any Segmentation Study

F. Segments versus Market Structures

G. Reasons for Segmentation

A. Introduction

Have you ever seen a product or service that truly appeals to everybody? If anything like this ever existed, it does not now. For decades, the most successful new products and services have focused on the needs of specific well-defined markets, or **market segments**. The vast majority of mid-size to large organizations no longer question the need to use market segmentation as a key part of their strategies.

Segmentation unfortunately can seem something of a mystery, in spite of all its value. It can look especially daunting to people new to this approach. One big problem is the overabundance of terminology surrounding segmentation. Procedures go by a wide variety of names, and many terms can point back to the same concepts. **Market segmentation** itself has had many names, including: regional marketing, micro marketing, niche marketing, and others. To make matters more confusing, writers sometimes will use these terms to mean something entirely different from segmentation.

This book aims to discuss market segmentation in standard English as much as possible. We will do our best to avoid "marketese," and will not fall back on complex equations or mathematical formulations—that's a promise.

At its core, segmentation is a completely logical and sensible way to approach a marketplace. A book about it should not be too much of a chore to read. Although we review statistical concepts, reading this book requires no advanced training. Wherever terms and procedures are introduced, you will find basic definitions nearby.

The discussion places special emphasis on:

- issues that you need to address in performing market segmentation,

- the procedures, and words surrounding them, that you may encounter in connection with segmentation, and,

- problems likely to arise in segmentation studies and ways around them.

This book falls broadly into two sections addressing different sets of concerns:

- **The first section**, chapters 1 and 2, talks about the basics and the terminology. This part is important if you need to cut through the jargon, if you are not that familiar with segmentation, or if you have taken part in a study that somehow fell short of goals.

- **The second section**, chapters 3 through 5, gives an overview of the methods and steps you need to take in a segmentation study. Sections 4 and 5 in particular provide unique information, showing what typically goes into a segmentation study and then reviewing the process step by step. We conclude with an annotated questionnaire used in a segmentation study.

These later chapters should serve as a check-list of steps and procedures, and likely will reveal some new approaches to segmentation that will help any study become more successful.

Finally, for readers somewhat rusty on the distinctions between types of data or variables we will discuss (binary, nominal, ordinal, interval, and ratio, as well as dependent versus independent), we have provided brief definitions in the Appendix.

(Revised for the fourth printing).

B. A Brief History

Segmentation in fact has a relatively short history as a formal discipline. Until the 1930s, econometric models held sway. These largely concerned themselves with price, and how products might get substituted as a function of price. They put such concerns as differences in benefits, communications, and promotions into a category called "non-price competition"—if they paid them any heed at all.

By the 1950s, the approach of most major manufacturers had shifted. They noticed that consumers can differ, but had little systematic knowledge of how. They now addressed their markets by a process of **product differentiation**. In this, manufacturers simply made as many different products as they could within their production or profit constraints. Then they sent these through their distribution systems.

They did this using the best marketing research insights available at that time. These had shown that, by varying products within a category, you could sell more products to more consumers.

This approach also made some sense in the market conditions of that time. New product categories were emerging and consumer demand exceeded supply. In this situation, buyers would pay extra for a novel and different product simply because of its newness, or perhaps simply to get any product of the new type. However, as categories matured, consumers' willingness to buy based solely on novelty diminished.

Perhaps because of the context in which it arose, **product differentiation** did not focus upon systematic understanding of consumer needs and wants. Rather, it looked inward, to the company's manufacturing and research and development (R&D) capabilities. This approach has also been called "the engineering way" to run a company. We can paraphrase this mind set briefly as: "If we can make it, they will buy it."

New products that emerged from this method would get "tested" either on stores' shelves or in expensive-to-run **test markets**. Products proliferated, with most of them expiring early in full-scale distribution. This approach obviously involved great inefficiency and so great cost.

The new products produced by this process sometimes differed only in surface or cosmetic ways. Some variations bordered on the ridiculous. You can find many such "innovations" as "the car with the city horn and country horn" in magazine advertisements from the product differentiation era.

Foolish **product differentiation** by no means has died, however. For instance, in the first printing we noted that the Wall Street Journal in December, 1990, reported on a new doll called "Steve the Tramp." Its manufacturer introduced it with catchy copy saying, "you smell him before you see him." They were among the many who had not learned that "different" does not always mean better. Lest we think things have gotten better, a quick search of the Web in 2013 revealed such real products as toilet paper wedding dresses, and a combined mp3 player and 50,000 volt taser (presumably so you can deter crime while playing your favorite tunes).

Although product differentiation did lead to some variations having genuine value, these did not emerge from systematic study of consumer needs. Rather, they most often came from intuition or gut feel. Those developing winning products often attributed their success to oracular vision and wisdom. Their competitors said it was due to luck. Whatever the case, the market did not define the process.

C. A Key Article

The first truly influential discussion of market segmentation as a concept did not appear until 1956. This article, Wendell R. Smith's "Product Differentiation and Market Segmentation As Alternative Marketing Strategies," still gets cited and quoted.

Smith voiced several positions never before systematically stated by any major writer on marketing. He rejected the classical economic theory of perfect competition, and in particular its assumptions of unvarying supply and demand. He pointed out that variety had become the norm in contemporary markets, among both those using and those supplying any class of product.

Smith also noted that product differentiation and segmentation have some similarities (both lead to different sets of products from a given manufacturer, for instance). However, they differed in one fundamental way: product differentiation strategies focused far less upon consumers' needs than did segmentation.

In a differentiation strategy, the manufacturer would try to make **something for everybody**, without in-depth study of any particular group within the market. Manufacturers took a global view, and then tried to make a wide variety of things. Smith compared product differentiation strategies to trying to take a **layer** of the marketing "cake" (cutting across all aspects of the market), and segmentation to taking a **slice** (by cutting vertically into one area of the marketplace).

Like trying to make something for everyone

As Smith said:

> *While successful product differentiation will result in. . . a horizontal share of a broad and generalized market, equally successful application of. . . market segmentation tends to produce depth of market position in the segments that are effectively defined and penetrated.*

In addition, Smith was the first to state that segmentation worked more efficiently than a strategy of simply producing as many products as possible. Creating different products only becomes effective *following* segmentation.

The truly successful organization must first find segments and then create products and services fitting their needs. Perhaps as much as anything in Smith's article, this idea signaled a new approach to consumers and markets.

Figure I: Evolving global approaches to the marketplace

Product differentiation

Attempts to vary market mix

Observed differences in responses to variations

Recognition that segments exist

Market segmentation

➤ No systematic product differences
➤ No variations in marketing mix
➤ Inward focus
➤ Reliance on intuition and anecdotes
➤ No apparent market segments

➤ Defined product differences
➤ Different marketing mixes
  ➤ Outward focus
➤ Uses systematic methods of investigation to create segments

D. Segmentation Basics

A key definition

Briefly stated, market segmentation identifies patterns of differences among groups in responses to communications, products and services.

The managerial assumption behind segmentation is that if segments:

1. Can be identified,
2. Can be described, and
3. Can be reached selectively and efficiently,

then the organization may increase sales and profits beyond those that can be obtained by assuming the market is homogeneous—by marketing to those segments (See, for instance., Green, Tull &Albaum, 1988).

These are the central ideas on which all segmentation is based. Still, these do not always appear in connection with the terms **segmentation** or **market segments.** These terms have become quite diffuse, largely through overuse. The word segment will be applied, often incorrectly, to any group showing patterns of similarity.

Key to the marketing definition of segments we find the idea that **these groups will have different patterns of responses in the marketplace.**

The segment where you are most likely to find your customers and prospects should differ strongly from other groups

E. Principal Questions for any Segmentation Study

1. Basic Approach

First we must consider the basic approach or philosophy used in defining segments. We can broadly divide segmentation into two sharply different classes:

- **Pre-determined ("a priori") segmentation**
- **Market-defined ("post hoc") segmentation**

These two diverge strongly in approach, intent, and basic philosophy.

Pre-determined ("a priori") segmentation, in most cases, involves selecting certain groups from a population and finding if they are segments. Too often, no actual investigation gets done. For instance, one could simply say that "people over 65," or "buyers of more than 5 packages of X last year" constitute segments

Market-defined ("post hoc") segmentation tries to identify segments based on actual market investigations, in particular, analysis of answers to survey questions intending to predict marketplace responses.

Wilkie (1971) proposed an alternative framework for distinguishing between segmentation approaches: **empirical** versus **product-stream**.

Much of the literature on market research refers to **empirical investigations**. In these reports, "segments" usually are groups of people defined by easily-found demographics or so-called "psychographics," or some readily observable behavior.

You might, for instance, encounter a study that first divides a market based on demographics, and then compares product usage rates for the various groups. Alternatively, you might see groups based on levels of product use, with other variables such as "psychographics," media habits, and demographics, used to describe the groups.

The second type of market segmentation uses **product-stream** methodologies. Wilkie proposed that this term mean any segmentation based on the **individual's perceptions and actions** in connection with a product. The focus here would be on collecting and examining detailed data on a respondent-by-respondent basis.

Myers & Tauber (1977) extended Wilkie's original definition to a more practical, but not 100% inclusive, form: product-stream methods are based on responses to any survey questionnaire items.

The key distinction then, is **whether we actually ask people to tell us about themselves, or if we infer who they are from outside sources.** When we frame the distinction in this way, we can see close parallels between the definitions of product-stream and post-hoc methods—and similarly, parallels between a priori and post hoc methods.

Many organizations find great appeal in the idea that we can divine all we need to know about people simply by observing their behavior (or stray facts that they leave on the Web, whether intentionally or not). This seems to lie at the core of much interest in data mining, and more recently **big data**. While it is undeniable that we can gain many insights from simply observing, it is questionable whether any method of gathering information that looks backward can help us to generate novel approaches or uncover genuinely new products, services, messages or appeals. **Post hoc segmentation** can do all these.

Some additional definitions of pre-determined (a priori) segmentation may help clarify its meaning and intentions.

A working definition:

> A priori segmentation occurs when the organization divides the market population into two or more groups **outside the scope of a research study**. Conducting a study will not influence the definition of the pre-defined segments.
>
> Some examples would include: segments consisting of brand loyal vs. brand switchers, segments based on SIC codes, or segments based on demographics.

From Green, Tull & Albaum (*Research for Marketing Decisions*):

> In [this] the researcher chooses some cluster-defining description in advance, such as respondent's favorite brand. Respondents are then classified into favorite-brand segments and further examined regarding their differences on other characteristics, such as demographics, or product benefits being sought.

From Myers & Tauber (*Market Structure Analysis*):

> A priori segmentation designates groups of consumers who are similar in terms of some factor of factors that are known or felt in advance to be related to product/service consumption; for example, demographics, psychographics, heavy vs. light usage, brand-loyalty.

Some alternative definitions of market-defined (post hoc) segmentation may further clarify the contrasts between this approach and market-defined methods.

A working definition:

> Post-hoc segmentation occurs after research has: (1) thoroughly analyzed the data, (2) determined that patterns differ considerably between two or more sub-groups found in the data, and (3) determined that these sub-groups can be consistently and concisely defined.

From Green, Tull & Albaum (*Research for Marketing Decisions*):

> Post hoc segmentation [occurs when] respondents are clustered according to the similarity of their multivariate profiles regarding such characteristics, not used in the original profile definition. In post hoc segmentation one does not know the number of clusters or their relative size until the cluster analysis has been completed.

From Myers & Tauber (*Market Structure Analysis*):

> In contrast [to a priori segmentation], response-based [market-defined] segmentation looks for patterns of product usage, attitudes, perceptions, and the like, that might hopefully signal useful market segments.

2. Common bases (or criteria) for defining segments

The number of possible bases for market-driven segmentation appears limitless. The sole restricting factors consist of problems at hand and the imaginations of the people trying to resolve these.

These are some possible bases for segmentation, including some that are used but not necessarily are the best possible ones. We will get to **preferred bases** shortly.

Product selection behaviors

Usage rates and occasions

Number of different brands used regularly

Knowledge of and experience with brands

Substitutability of related categories

Brand selection behaviors

Favorite brand(s)

Acceptable brands

Disliked brands

Brand loyalty vs. brand switching

Product class-related attitudes

Benefits sought

Problems encountered using product

Attribute utilities of brand

Unmet product-related needs

Brand-related attitudes

Brand awareness and understanding

Brand-related perceptions

Brand user imagery

Perceived appropriateness for use occasions

Person-related attitudes

Self-perceptions

Other "psychographics"

"Life styles"

Other interests and activities

Other bases

Stage in life cycle

Socioeconomic status

Ethnicity

Other demographics

Adapted from Green, Tull & Albaum (1988).

F. Segments vs. Market Structures

Just as markets can contain many groups that are not segments, they can contain many others structures that are not segments (Myers & Tauber 1977). A market structure could, for instance, consist of relationships between groups of products/services. You could find such patterns based upon ways respondents find products to present similar or dissimilar benefits or problems. You could also group products based on respondents' perceptions and associated imagery.

Some extensive segmentation studies may use methodologies to determine both segments and other structures.

A multidimensional map (sometimes called a "perceptual map") that showed just the relationship of products, and not any consumer groups, would show a **market structure** but no market segments. One such map appears below.

You may see **structural** analyses referred to as either **perceptual** or **preference mapping** in the literature. Now the term perceptual mapping is applied to many techniques that represent individuals' or groups' opinions (or actions, as for instance, in brand choices) graphically. We will discuss mapping again in Section IV—E.

Figure 2: Structural "Perceptual" Map

Note: Brands are closest to the attributes with which they had the strongest associations

G. Reasons for Segmentation

In theory, any market of sufficient size could be segmented profitably. However, without research it is impossible to tell in advance whether this will become a reality. The pertinent first question may well be whether the market seems to warrant doing any research.

Clearly, though, some situations favor finding true segments in a previously unsegmented market. **Salient change** in the marketplace often signals the need to segment or re-segment populations. Evidence of changes like any of the following can justify trying segmentation.

1. Groups emerge for which new (different) products, positioned properly, can have real meaning

Apple, as is well known, developed a personal computer differing in some particulars from the IBM personal computer (PC). However, once the early days were over, these differences were subtle, largely in details of operating systems and methods of handling data storage. Apple computers in objective comparisons since the 1990s, never have held any large functional advantage over IBM-compatible PCs. Even by this early date, IBM-compatible PC users could get software allowing their machines to match closely the look and feel of the Apple (Macintosh)—even if they at first had to search diligently for it.

You would never know this from the positioning of the Apple computer, or in fact from nearly all who have selected an Apple over an IBM-based PC. Apple always portrayed its computers as "for the rest of us," "friendly," and supremely "easy to use."

As the market for PCs grew, Apple found the segment of users who did not want complexity in their personal computers, who wanted something easy to use out of the box, without anything to add or change. This approach has given Apple a consistent history of profits that are the envy of most in the computer hardware industry. Apple consistently has been able to charge higher prices and to generate higher margins than nearly any maker of IBM-compatible personal computers.

There was an interesting shift in the years just before 2000, when Windows started doing a reasonable job emulating the Apple look and feel. Apple responded by sharply lowering prices—but not all the way to the level of PCs. Even as more distinctions diminished, Apple held a consistent but narrow price edge in PCs. This has continued in more recent years as their new-product focus shifted to devices as well as PCs. In pursuing these newer markets, Apple continued to show the power of finding a segment and positioning a product as filling its unmet needs.

2. Relatively under-served groups emerge in the market. They have enough potential to justify a new approach to products/services

Honda's studies of the car market led them to believe there could be room for another entry in the luxury price range. They isolated and learned about the segment likely to buy cars of this type. This group differed sharply from traditional Honda buyers. We do not generally think of luxury car buyers as underserved, but at the time Honda did indeed see an opportunity in this market.

Honda introduced the Acura as a result. Honda's research showed that the virtues of the Honda name to traditional Honda buyers did not hold for luxury car buyers. Approaching the market for truly expensive cars would likely require an entirely separate brand having its own identity.

Nearly everything in the marketing of the Acura differs from Honda's traditional practices. They advertise and promote the two brands differently, and usually do not even sell them in the same place. These differences in marketing mix reflect what Honda learned about the perceptions held by the luxury-car buyer segment.

3. Specialized competitors emerge, forcing the firm to narrow its focus onto more tightly defined markets

Sears for many years has struggled to retain a retailing business in both "hard" and "soft" goods. This in part came about because around 1970 to 1980, large chains such as Home Depot and Best Buy, specializing in hardware and appliances, began to develop strong national presences. These were tough and focused competitors who did not have to address the many markets and concerns that Sears did.

In contrast, Target stores rose to national prominence in large part by (as their name suggests) taking a more targeted approach. They actually are an outgrowth of the Dayton Hudson Dry Goods stores, an old-line business with an identity once similar to Sears. Target around 1960 made the hard decision not to be all things to all people. Instead they concentrated on being what they termed an "upscale discount store," and concentrated on selling "soft goods," such as apparel and housewares, with any eye toward designer flare. They avoided selling major appliances and had a relatively modest assortment of hardware. While recessions and further market shifts have proven hard for all retailers, over decades Target has continued with far fewer problems than Sears, which adhered to a strategy of trying to sell nearly everything.

4. Major differences emerge between purchasers of competitive products in a product class

Beers differ in objective fact, but among the major brands, perhaps do as much so in users' perceptions. Alcoholic beverages fulfill a complex set of social and psychological needs—which, fascinating as they are, fall beyond the scope of this book. Still, there is no argument that tastes in beer have evolved. Not that long ago, imported or craft beers accounted for a tiny fraction of all beers consumed in the US, with the vast majority of all consumption being some form of pale lager.

The makers of Coors, one of those pales, were quite interested in ensuring that their beer would compete effectively among the more dominant brands. As they investigated this possibility, they discovered an emerging group that wanted a beer darker and fuller than domestic beers—and perhaps something more exotic—but still not as dark as the then dominant import, Guinness Stout.

And so George Killian and his red Irish ale both were born. Not to disillusion any readers, but the ale itself was first brewed in the part of Ireland known as Colorado,[1] and as for George himself, he amounts to no more than a fond figment of the collective imaginings of an advertising agency,

Whatever its beginnings, red Irish ale definitely appeals to a new segment of beer drinkers who want something more than their usual beers. And George, imaginary or not, has sold a respectable quantity of beer pursuing this segment of beer drinkers.

---

[1] For those who are not 100% sure of their geography, Colorado in fact is located where it has been for many years, between Utah and Kansas.

II. Approaching Segmentation: First Considerations and Steps

A. The First Necessity: Managerial Involvement in Segmentation

B. The Baseline Segmentation Study: Characteristics

C. Ongoing Segmentation Studies: Characteristics

D. Types of Variables Used in Segmentation

E. Considerations in Selecting Bases for Segmentation

F. Considerations in Selecting Descriptor Variables

G. Pre-determined (A Priori) Segmentation: Some Further Considerations

H. Market Driven (Post Hoc) Segmentation Methods

A. The First Necessity: Managerial Involvement

I. Why management needs to become involved

Market segmentation involves understanding and finding groups that have the most need for a product or service, and can influence service or product delivery, communications and even new product development. All of these considerations mean it should become **a key element in an organization's strategy**.

Unfortunately, the term **strategy**, like segmentation, has received considerable misuse. Strictly speaking, a strategy is no less than a corporation's overall plan for doing business, a template that shapes many of its actions and behavior.

Tactics are not synonymous with strategy. Rather, tactics are the specific means which a corporation employs as it tries to meet its goals. To use the common sports analogy, tactics would be about winning the game and strategy would be about coming out first for the whole season.

Because of its role in shaping corporate strategy, segmentation needs support from the very top of the organization. This must then follow through most of the organization. For instance:

- The firm's marketing organization must be able to put in place new or modified marketing strategies and, as needed, vary pricing, promotion, and distribution;

- R&D may need to devise product variations, and manufacturing must be able to produce those variations;

- Finance could be required to report costs, profits and margins by market segment; and

- Market research will need to monitor and measure changes in perceptions and perhaps ultimately purchaser response by segment—and provide feedback to the organization as is needed.

In addition, market segmentation requires constancy and consistency to work properly. It is not just the study. Rather, it is a continuing process of applying segmentation to all marketing.

Not involving the key stake-holders, including those in top management, remains one of the leading reasons for the failure of marketing segmentation efforts. Too often, people in key positions—including those who would be strongly affected by the actions arising from a segmentation study—express surprise in the final presentation at seeing what has been done—or worse, even that a study has been done at all. These are the kinds of surprises we definitely want to avoid.

2. Getting top management involved

As all of these considerations may make plain, the final decisions on how to use the insights and guidance from segmentation studies must, in most cases, come from an organization's top management. That is, it comes from people other than the market researchers and marketers who actually perform the study.

Nobody has yet devised a certain way to ensure approval. Top management in the organization must have some degree of willingness to do segmentation before the subject of a new approach ever gets broached with them. Of course, if the directive to segment the market comes from on high, this drops a key barrier. But this by no means makes it sure that the project will be well received by the time it gets done.

Creating a sense of ownership and involvement in top management is crucial for the acceptance and use of segmentation results. In too many cases, researchers finally win approval—perhaps after lengthy personal selling to upper management—and then disappear for weeks or months until the findings come out. By then, top management may not have a good sense of what the project intends to find—and may even find it hard to believe that they agreed to do it as it finally got done.

You can help to bypass this problem in two ways. First and most apparently, remember to keep management informed about segmentation studies. Then, as much as possible, involve them in any decisions along the way.

If management does not want to know anything along the way, you may need to do more selling. If this does not work, perhaps you could consider doing a tracking study instead.

They need to get involved even if they aren't always very forward-looking

B. Types of Segmentation Studies: The Baseline Study

The **baseline study** refers to a corporation's first try at segmenting a market in a given way. Implicit in the term **baseline** is the idea that this initial segmentation will be repeated at some time, and the results from the studies compared. This may not be that common in practice since so much effort is involved. Studies may not get repeated for a good number of years. Therefore this description usually applies to that one big study that the organization may do.

Some characteristics generally associated with baseline studies follow:

- Base-line studies typically are broad-based. They usually sample from both current users and prospects, while investigating responses to current and perhaps proposed products/services.

- They use large samples and large numbers of variables, to analyze and compare alternative segmentation bases.

- They use variables developed with the intent that these could get included in a classification or scoring model. (That is, they use variables suitable for measurement in later studies).

  ◊ Some otherwise solid segmentation efforts have been frustrated by using variables that cannot be reproduced in a scoring model (or typing tool).

  ◊ A scoring model typically is a short subset of questions from the original study, which could be restricted to as few as 10 items (and rarely fewer) —depending on intentions in how these variables are going to be used.

  ◊ In any event, variables that typically do not get included in a later study might arise from a special analytical method, such as **conjoint analysis** or **maximum difference scaling** (also called **MaxDiff)** trade-off exercise. These exercises can be too long to include in a later study that has additional goals.

    - We will discuss these concerns in more detail later.

- Baseline studies entail substantial time invested in the data analysis section of the study, for exploring alternative segmentation bases, alternative algorithms and alternative classification models.

- They typically involve considerable expense, due to extensive planning, large samples, consideration of many variables, and long and detailed analysis.

C. Types of Segmentation Studies: The Ongoing Study

Additional segmentation studies conducted to support or take advantage of a completed baseline segmentation generally get called **ongoing segmentation studies.**

In their fullest form, these more or less replicate the baseline study—taking into account any learning that would help refine the next effort or new variables to reflect new marketplace conditions. However, follow-up studies come in many types, and can be done for many reasons, including:

- confirming or adjusting (fine tuning) established segments;

- describing established segments in more detail;

- answering specific managerial and/or marketing questions, analyzed by segment;

- more rarely, segmenting a baseline segment further (sometimes called second stage segmentation) using a different set of basis variables (for example, investigating one or two segments from an earlier study and splitting them further).

Many ongoing segmentation studies, however, could be considered **pre-determined (a priori)** segmentation, if the baseline study generates a classification model that places respondents into their proper segments in the following studies or waves.

In such ongoing studies, respondents do not get analyzed by a new segmentation procedure. Rather, they get **scored** into groups based on criteria developed in the baseline study. This often gets done by use of discriminant analysis, as shown in Section IV - I.

A good spot for ongoing study

D. Basic Types of Variables Used in Segmentation Studies

Segmentation studies almost always include two basic types of variables: often called **basis** and **descriptor** variables.

Basis variables, as their name shows, form the **basis** of segmentation—that is, these variables will be used with the method chosen to group people into segments. Several considerations determine the extent to which you will know these as you start a study.

- For baseline studies, you most likely will not want to specify the exact basis variables beforehand. Rather, you most likely will start with a wider set of variables and narrow these by finding which work best to differentiate groups in meaningful ways.

- For pre-determined (a priori) segmentation, basis variables may often get specified by (for instance) senior management.

- For post-baseline (ongoing) studies, the basis variables often may be specified by a classification model from the baseline study.

Descriptor variables help in characterizing and differentiating among the segments, and can lead to actions. Some examples of these include:

- Demographics,

- Life cycle characteristics,

- Media usage,

- Hobbies and outside interests,

- Web habits.

These descriptors will serve to make the segments **selectively reachable**, particularly in terms of media and Web habits, and may also help shape the message.

Selection of useful descriptors, as much as selection of good basis variables, is critical to creating a study that can be applied successfully. A study that finds out a great deal about what different segments think and do, but cannot efficiently find those segments, becomes just an "interesting" piece of work, not a useful one.

Unfortunately, probably not a place to get basis variables

E. Considerations in Selecting the Bases for Segmentation

1. Basics

The selection of the basis variables is the one of the most critical decisions in any segmentation study. We may have some good ideas about what might go into this set, but certainty is rare. Therefore, researchers often will include a wide selection of possible basis variables in a baseline survey.

No demonstrably "best" set of variables (as a basis for segmentation) exists in any situation. Certainly, we have nothing like a mathematical "proof" to determine the best solution. Too many possible alternatives present themselves in any situation, and situations differ in too many ways from each other for "hard and fast" rules to be laid down.

Still, we have observed that either *too few basis variables or too much dissimilarity among basis variables can lead to poor results.* This suggests several guidelines for constructing a more "disaster-proof" questionnaire, as follows:

> Include at least one battery of questions addressing the concerns that you believe will form the basis for grouping respondents.

> Including a good number of pertinent questions, if possible more than one battery, with each taking a different approach, provides some insurance.

For instance, you might include:

- one battery about product use patterns and preferences and
- one battery dealing with ways respondents view the product and reasons or occasions for its use, and/or
- another battery about user and self-perceptions related to the category, and /or
- another battery addressing broader "life-style" and interest-related concerns.

You would then use selected questions from the various batteries that lead to the most sensible—and of course useable—segment definitions.

However, it is best to try not to include too many different types of questions in the basis variables. In theory, you can divide the marketplace by including simultaneously (in the basis) attitudes, use patterns, awareness, perceptions, demographics, media habits, other interests, leisure activities, etc. In practice, such diversity rarely produces good results (see, e.g., Myers & Tauber, 1976).

You will usually do better keeping **location-oriented** variables, such as demographics, media usage, etc., out of the basis variables—as the next section describes.

Strategic planning concerns should play a key role in selecting basis variables. For instance, you might consider a different segmentation approach when facing strong price competition than when facing extensive brand switching or rapid technical product changes. Nonetheless, some writers have suggested certain variables as **preferred** or better in certain broadly defined situations. One such list follows.

2. Some "preferred" bases for segmentation studies

Given all the possible basis variables you might use, questions can arise as to which work best with different study goals. The list below shows the basics that could appear in several types of studies. It is by no means exhaustive. Each heading below may itself seem clear and evident. However, many studies will try to address several of these concerns at once. In that case, balancing the basic requirements of each area of inquiry can become difficult.

Referring to a list such as this can help determine whether studies with multiple goals are too ambitious. Many such lists have been developed. This one, from quite a few years back, still serves well.

For studies providing a general understanding of a market:

Benefits sought;

Needs the product will fill (needs and perceived benefits may not be synonymous);

Product purchase and usage patterns;

Brand loyalty and switching patterns.

For studies of pricing decisions:

Price sensitivity, by purchase and usage patterns;

Product, user and self-images associated with products at different prices;

Product usage patterns;

Sensitivity to "deals."

For studies focusing on product/service positioning:

Product usage;

Product preferences;

Benefits sought;

Needs the products will fill;

Product-, user-, and self-perceptions.

For advertising decisions:

Benefits sought;

Needs;

Psychographics/ "life styles";

Product-, user-, and self-perceptions.

For studies of new product concepts (and introduction):

Reaction to new concepts (intention to buy, preference over current brand, etc.);

Benefits sought;

Product usage patterns;

Price sensitivity.

(Adapted from Wind & Claycamp, 1976)

For distribution decisions:

Store loyalty and patronage;

Benefits sought in store selection;

Sensitivity to "deals."

F. Considerations in Selecting Descriptor Variables

Selection of a basis for segmentation may be either straightforward or very difficult. However, selection of variables as descriptors of the segments is almost always complex. This complexity stems from a number of factors.

1. **The number of possible descriptor variables is enormous**

   Most of the variables covered in the consumer behavior literature can be considered as segment descriptors. At some time each probably has.

   It is possible to become lost in all these possible descriptors, both for those who design the study, and for the respondents who answer a survey.

2. **Often links are questionable between basis and descriptor variables**

   Depending on the descriptors you choose, you may not be able to identify segments with varying responses to marketing actions. This often proves to be the case with demographic and other general customer characteristics.

   Conversely, although groups defined by such characteristics, demographics in particular, tend to be easily described, they often do not have varying responses to marketing variables—and so are not true segments.

   This lack of strong connections can emerge even in well-designed studies, although with the ways of locating connections outlined in the section on profiling segments, this is quite uncommon. Certainly, if investigations stop at the level of cross-tabulated tables, then usage, attitudes and opinions typically will cut fairly evenly across demographic characteristics.

   You may have trouble locating segments with differing **life-styles**, although life-styles sometimes look like demographics. Life-style is a loosely defined term, and as such these characteristics may or may not have some relation to product use. Unfortunately, life styles and simple demographics often have few close correspondences. This is shown anecdotally but convincingly by differences among people living in the same neighborhood, or even the same block. While their demographics may be quite similar, their ways of viewing themselves, leisure activities, and interests—and so their life-styles may vary sharply.

3. **Doing something ("actionability") always remains a difficult question**

   Inadequate descriptors can lead to a study in which you develop some strong-looking insights from the basis variables, but not enough action-oriented information to move forward with any real confidence. During study design, consider management's ability to use the findings, in particular information from the descriptors. Will these help form the firm's marketing strategy and tactics (for instance, can they influence media scheduling, distribution, communications, and so on)?

   Good choices of descriptor variables, including variables that can be used to locate audiences effectively, is critical. Getting this right can make the difference between a study that forms the basis of an organization's actions and a study that sits in drawer

G. Pre-Determined (A Priori) Methods in More Detail

1. Common a prior bases

Pre-determined segmentation schemes get frequent use, especially because organizations can often perform it with little or no expense and time devoted to primary research. Bases used for pre-determined (**a priori**) segmentation vary widely depending upon goals. Some of these bases might include the following:

- Users versus non-users, or heavy vs. medium vs. light users (this has the advantage of providing "instant segments" if you can selectively appeal to each group)

- Brand loyal versus brand switchers,

- Under 35 versus 35 and older,

- Innovators versus followers,

- East Coast versus Midwest versus West Coast,

- "High" versus "mid" versus "low" income groups,

- Pre-defined "values"-based groups appended to data files, by such services as VALS or PRIZM,[1]

- Groups based on the organizations "cost centers" or "profit centers,"

A real example shows how strongly **a priori** segmentation can limit thinking and lead nowhere. This a priori way of dividing up the world of clinical depression represents a mix of inward-gazing and not much thinking:

- Segment 1:   Mild or moderate depression
- Segment 2:   Severe depression
- Segment 3:   Depression with anxiety
- Segment 4:   Bi-polar
- Segment 5:   Treatment resistant depression.

What exactly can we derive from this classification?

- ☞ People with severe depression are more depressed than people with mild or moderate depression;

- ☞ People who are depressed with anxiety can be put into any of several other segments;

- ☞ Come to think of it, so can people with "treatment resistant" depression.

Missing of course, is any sense of how to treat these segments differently (indeed nearly impossible with the strong overlaps) and any insight into the true differences among those suffering with this problem.

---

[1] VALS and PRIZM are trademarked names for services that have assigned a group or personality type to many of the households in the US. They match households to groups based on demographics and neighborhood characteristics. These groups can be purchased along with other household demographics and appended to survey data files.

2. When is it appropriate to use pre-determined segmentation?

While pre-determined or a prior segmentation in many situations does more harm than good, it sometimes is the only or best recourse. You might consider this in any of the situations described below.

Study goals include exploring or understanding differences between known segments.

For instance: Explore in depth why women rarely send flowers to men

Determine why more affluent households do not spend more on state lotteries.

Previous research has revealed segments that you can re-use.
Usually, after a baseline segmentation study, all further research on the segments includes re-classifying respondents into segments by the same scheme used in the baseline study.

For instance: Determine the how perceptions of our low-priced brand have shifted among the five segments defined two years ago, in the baseline study.

You have a "pre-segmentation" algorithm available and believe it will provide actual segments.

For instance: Find which predefined segmentation group (provided by services such as VALS or PRIZM), if any, your brand low-priced brand might appeal to the most.

Another VALS well before PCs

In this case, the segments derived by VALS (or PRIZM) form the basis for the analysis. Again, the intent of these groups is to delineate segments of the population that differ in life style or "psychographic" characteristics. You do not need any original research to assign households to VALS or PRIZM groups. As noted, you can, for instance, purchase lists of households and neighborhoods broken down into these groups. Households usually get assigned to these groups based on their socioeconomic characteristics and characteristics of their zip codes or block groups.

When there are no other bases for market-driven segmentation, e.g., for emerging product categories.

For instance: What software products and services do personal computer users who have respectively mouse-driven and touch-screen computers use most often?

Here the type of computer owned forms the basis for segmentation. The market here is so volatile that you might use the type of computer to stand for market divisions based on more thorough knowledge of prospects and users.

A study like this could qualify as segmentation if you did it expecting to find strong behavioral differences between owners of these types of personal computers.

3. Some cautions on pre-determined (a priori) segmentation

Sometimes a truism bears repeating: Our society has been, and remains, dynamic. Segmentation schemes developed three or four years ago may not remain appropriate today. In all likelihood, the world has changed in some ways that will influence nearly any product or service category. The proper way to check this is to keep investigating the market, testing segments periodically to check their stability.

Definitions of pre-determined (**a priori**) segments may, in fact, prove to be highly unstable. For instance, consider heavy computer users versus light users today, compared with five years ago. The nature of each segment has shifted to include strongly different types of individuals. For instance, even five years ago, most heavy users had some technical expertise, while today that does not hold. If we include tablets among computers, then the heaviest users may know very little about how their devices work indeed. Similarly, even today's light users can use equipment that only the most advanced users would have had then--and so on.

Although it is theoretically possible to use **a priori** or pre-defined groups including either demographic or life-style information to develop real segments (as we just discussed), too often these get substituted for segmentation genuinely connected with the product or service. Off-the-shelf ways of dividing the market should never substitute for serious thought and investigation. Segmenting a market incorrectly can be worse than treating it as one mass market.

Perhaps the strongest caveat against pre-determined segmentation comes from how easily it aids and abets ossified management traditions, low research budgets, and lazy thinking.

Not our type of "a priori" (Emmanuel Kant discussing "a priori" before we had the wonderful world of statistics)

H. Market-Driven (Post Hoc) Segmentation Methods: More Detail

1. Methods for segmentation vs. investigation of other market structures

Recalling that not all market structures are market segments (Myers & Tauber, 1977), some multivariate methods work better in investigating market segments and some work better in examining other structures. A brief layout (or taxonomy) of methods, with some common names that you may encounter—and some not so common—follows directly below. Subsequent sections will discuss each of the segmentation methods in detail.

Methods used for segmentation:

- Cluster analysis (most often used)
  - Hierarchical
  - Aggregation (or agglomeration) models
  - Disaggregation (or divisive) models.
  - Iterative (optimizing) methods
- Newer methods, including TwoStep, latent class, spectral fuzzy and EM clustering—and many others.
- Automatic interaction detection (CHAID) and Classification and Regression Trees (CRT) and extensions
  - CHAID and related methods (e.g., C4.5, C5.0, J48, etc.)
  - CRT and related methods (CART, C&RT, QUEST etc.)
  - Extensions including random forests and adaptive bootstrapping
- Model-based methods including finite mixture models (FIMIX) and some types of latent class analysis
- Correspondence analysis or dual scaling.
- Q-Type factor analysis (essentially discredited).

"Hybrid" techniques for segmentation:

- Conjoint analysis-based, MaxDiff-based or discrete choice model-based clustering (clustering on individual partial utilities);
- R-Type factor analysis-based clustering (that is, clustering on individual factor scores of product attribute ratings).

Techniques for investigating other market structures (especially, multivariate mapping):

- Discriminant analysis;
- Multidimensional scaling techniques;
- Correspondence analysis (dual scaling) and biplots.

2. Some cautions on market driven (post hoc) segmentation

You cannot know several key facts until you analyze the data, in particular the number and size of segments. This is inevitable because segments must emerge from patterns of similarity and dissimilarity among respondents.

Unfortunately, none of us can "intuit" how results coming from responses to many question items will group respondents. Therefore, we cannot readily determine how many segments these imply.

Other information does not emerge until after the analysis; this includes:

- the extent of segment stability and segment homogeneity; and

- the size and complexity of classification models that may emerge from the segmentation.

Faulty models leading to poor segmentation results always remain a possibility, and have been reported anecdotally. However, your author has not seen a market impossible to segment, where those involved followed the basic guidelines set out by Young, Ott and Feigin (1978—see Section III-I for particulars) for which markets can be segmented. This is based on experience and reporting gathered over 25 years. Still, it is prudent to recall that you cannot know if a model works until you try it.

You can follow several strategies that will sharply increase the likelihood of getting useful results. Later sections of this book will discuss steps to take as well as some common pitfalls, and what you can do to avoid them.

Finally, some practitioners unfortunately get into serious trouble by underestimating the complexity of segmentation data, and as a result, leaving too little time for the analysis needed.

As can happen with any long study, pressures may arise to promise early delivery and to hasten the analysis. A segmentation study is one place where you should try never to rush the data analysis and interpretation.

A segmentation study can start to feel like handling one of these

PART 2: METHODS AND SPECIFIC STEPS TO TAKE

III. SEGMENTATION RESEARCH DESIGN

A. Selecting the Segmentation Approach

B. Selecting the Unit of Analysis

C. Determining Sample Design

D. Considering and Testing Data Reliability

E. Validation and Validity

F. Segment Stability

G. Determining Segment Homogeneity

H. Segmentation Methods and Their "Optimization" Criteria

I. Dealing with a Difficult to Segment Market

J. Validity: Some Methods for Approaching this Unresolved Question

K. Designing Data Collection Instruments: Cost Considerations

L. Recap of the Basic Segmentation Issues

A. Selecting the Segmentation Approach

Once your organization decides to segment a market, you must select a basic set of analytical tools or algorithms. These fall into several broad classes. Each of the ones widely used in market segmentation makes certain assumptions about the data type and/or type of measures. You need to know the strengths and limitations of each analytical tool, and to keep these in mind while designing the remainder of the study.

Through the 1970s, the nature of the data limited choices of algorithms much more sharply than it does now. (For instance, Wind & Claycamp [1976] saw the entire research design as closely dependent on the analytical tools used.)

Most often, one of these types of methods gets used.

Cluster analysis

Most clustering procedures require interval-scaled variables. You cannot use "nominal"-level data or yes/no responses, without further work, in the most widely used clustering routines. This means that clustering usually gets based on scaled questions and direct measurements (volume consumed, packages used, age, income, and so on). Procedures typically classed as clustering do not have a "dependent" variable (that is, a variable identifying some set of groups that you hope the segmentation will contrast).

Model driven methods

Newer methods such as latent class analysis, finite mixture (or FIMIX) models used with partial least squares (PLS) regression and Bayesian networks can generate segmentation schemes based on a model of how variables relate to each other. Strong successes have been reported with all of these, but the partial least squares method is restricted to the same types of variables as in a regular regression. The other methods can accept many types of variables.

Automatic interaction detection: CHAID and CRT and related methods

A.I.D. stands for **automatic interaction detection**, because the tree-like patterns of relationships among variables that it generates can clearly capture complex patterns of **interactions**—the ways that variables depend on each other to lead to some outcome (such as volume of use or membership in a group). A.I.D. itself is long gone, but its many descendants, starting with **CHAID**, follow the same basic approach. All require you to designate a dependent variable. This variable serves as the basis for separating people into a set of groups that you want to contrast. These procedures split the sample and then split it again, finding more tightly defined (and smaller) subgroups. For a time debates flared in the statistical community about whether **CRT**-related or CHAID-related methods worked better—but all have evolved now to become very powerful methods.

Concerning data limitations, open-ended, verbatim responses seldom get used as basis variables, no matter what the analytical technique. This happens mainly for practical reasons. These responses simply become too difficult to handle. Great complexity arises in attempting to capture and collapse many shades of meaning into numeric codes. Open-ends also can prove surprisingly prone to errors or inaccuracy in coding.

Similarly, questions that use the so called **multi-punch** (or **multiple response**) format do not lend themselves to multivariate analyses. Only specialized techniques, such as CHAID, can handle this type of data, and that only by combining responses and discerning patterns in the combinations.

B. Selecting the Unit of Analysis

Segmentation studies often work with the assumption that the unit of analysis will be the individual. However, this is not always correct. For instance, studies of financial behavior often need to focus on the behavior of the entire household.

When the **unit of analysis** becomes more than one individual, definitions must become explicit. For instance, you can define "household" in many ways, such as:

- total household,
- income earners only,
- those influential in the purchase only, and
- other combinations.

When several individuals get involved in a decision, you must take care to collect and to balance properly the opinions of all. As many such multiple-respondent studies have shown, interviewing only one influential person often will lead to distorted results. Most people estimate their own influence on any given decision as quite strong, and others as less influential.

You may also find multi-person sampling units in commercial organizations. Some of these might include: groups of purchasing agents, purchasing engineers or the purchasing committee, the senior financial officers (controller, CFO, treasurer, etc.), sales or calling officers, marketing executives, etc.

Other entities, not at all similar to individuals, can become sampling units. Examples would include:

- sales territories,
- zip codes or other geographical entities,
- corporate departments.

The use of multi-person units of analysis poses some distinctive problems in data analysis and sampling statistics. Wind, (1978) addresses these in a more traditional way in "Issues and Advances in Segmentation Research."

Multiple units of analysis may cause us to consider use of the relatively new set of methods falling under the heading of **multilevel analysis**, to make sure we are partitioning out the variability of responses correctly. Multilevel analysis is quite powerful and can address many problems where sampling units are linked. A detailed discussion of this method is well beyond our scope here—it would require an entire book of its own. You can find a basic—and reasonably priced—primer on this in the references.

C. Determining Sample Design

All true segmentation studies have one goal in common: using the segmentation found among the entire pertinent market. Therefore, in theory, these studies require probability samples from that market to function as well as possible. Quota samples seldom work well in segmentation studies if the goal is estimating overall usage among all households or all users of a certain type.

Post data-collection sample balancing procedures, or *weighting*, can severely affect results you get from clustering procedures. These also make it difficult to estimate errors, and they complicate modeling of the segments. Sampling entails many steps. It is actually a highly complex process; it is easy to underestimate the technical acumen, thought and effort this entails. The chart below reviews, in broad strokes, the key steps.

STEP	DESCRIPTION
1. Define the population	Could get defined by (a) "elements," or kinds of people, (b) where (place), and (c) when (time).
2. Specify sampling frame	Determine lists or sources for locating the sample--for example, using the telephone book, a city directory, random digit dialing (RDD) in specified area, recruiting at a mall, etc.
3. Specify sampling unit	Specify the "unit" for sampling. The unit might be one person, a household, an entire city block, or a company. The sampling unit may contain one or many "elements" in a population.
4. Specify sampling method	Determine the method by which the sampling units are to be selected (e.g., RDD, every N adults entering a store, etc.).
5. Determine sample size	Choose the number within the population to be sampled.
6. Specify the sampling plan	Choose the procedures for selecting the sampling units.
7. Select the sample	Carry out office and field work necessary for the selection of the sample

Figure 3: Alternative global sampling frames that do not fit

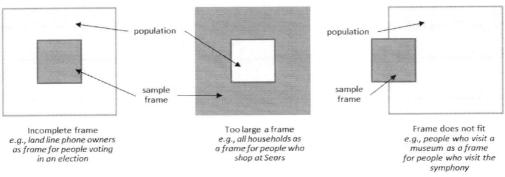

Incomplete frame	Too large a frame	Frame does not fit
e.g., land line phone owners as frame for people voting in an election	e.g., all households as a frame for people who shop at Sears	e.g., people who visit a museum as a frame for people who visit the symphony

(Adapted from: Green, Tull & Albaum [1988]).

D. Considering and Testing Data Reliability

A question may arise about whether methods or data are "reliable." **Reliability**, as used statistically, often gets applied to scaled measurements. Then it simply means the extent to which results would be consistent if the scale were used again.

Reliability can refer to two types of consistency. The first is whether results would remain the same if the same individuals were "tested" and "retested" with the same questions. The second is consistency between groups of similar respondents.

Determining **reliability** is not the same as investigating **validity**. The validity of a measurement refers to how closely it in fact reflects some "reality." However, since a non-reliable measurement cannot be valid, reliability puts an upper limit on validity. As follows, validity is the much more difficult of the two to assess.

Several alternative approaches to reliability estimation exist in the social sciences. **None of these** methods gets much use in market research, largely due to practical considerations. These are the principal ways in which reliability gets measured:

- **Test-retest reliability** involves applying the same measure to the same objects (or respondents) a second time. Because of increasing difficulty of completing even one study in market research, this form of investigation remains quite rare.

- **Alternative-forms reliability** involves measuring the same objects by two instruments designed to be as nearly alike as possible. Generally, only one form gets used in market research. In some surveys, differences between versions may consist solely of "rotation" of items to reduce "position bias." This is not at all the same as using alternative forms that contain different questions.

-
  Internal-comparison reliability involves comparing responses among the various items on a multiple item battery, in which several questions are designed to measure the same thing. However, the batteries of scaled items used in market research intend to measure many related concerns (unlike the items on an intelligence test). This concept therefore has little application in analysis of nearly any market survey.

One of these must be right

E. Validation and Validity

Some confusion surrounds these two terms, particularly in connection with segmentation. As mentioned, aside from some specialized statistical meanings, **validity** remains largely an abstract notion, concerned with the extent to which findings reflect "the truth." Little can be done to demonstrate "validity" convincingly; as close as most market researchers will come (if that) is learning whether findings "work" as **they get applied**.

As a reminder, the fact that something seemingly works does not prove the truth of its view of reality. As an extreme example, some folk medicines hit fortuitously upon treatments for diseases although they had incorrect explanations for the mechanisms causing the disease.

You may see the term "validation" in connection with discriminant analysis, and sometimes in association with clustering. It is sometimes called "split-sample" or "hold out" validation. This is because it involves dividing the sample into two (or more) random subsamples, subjecting one sub-sample to a procedure, and then checking the results in the other ("hold-out") sub-sample.

With discriminant analysis, a sub-sample would be "held out," and the rest of the sample put through the procedure. The "classification scheme" generated by this analysis would then be tried on the hold-out sample. Then the extent to which this scheme worked correctly would be calculated.

You can use clusters (or market segments) in a "split-sample validation" approach. As we will describe in later sections, you would apply discriminant analysis to a portion of the sample. Then you would calculate the extent to which the analysis correctly predicts cluster (or segment) membership.

Other methods of validation also have been devised, some very powerful, but these are yet to be included most software packages.

Sometimes the answers are not that easy

F. Investigating Segment Stability

1. Basic considerations

Segments have little meaning if they do not maintain an identity over a reasonable amount of time, and over a reasonable range of situations. The meaning of "reasonable," of course, remains open to question. However, segmentation entails enough effort that fair consistency about two years seems a minimum expectation for a useful solution. Stability in fact involves three related issues:

- Segment stability **over time** (will respondents still select the same brand of beer most often two years from now?)

- Segment stability **over situations** (will respondents select the same brand of beer for a fishing trip as for at home?)

- Segment stability **over times of the year** (will respondents select the same beer brands in March as in August?)

2. Major factors affecting segment stability

The specificity of the basis for segmentation

More general bases for segmentation (such as benefits sought from the product category, or needs) usually produce more stable segments. Similarly, more specific bases for segmentation (such as price sensitivity, or adherence to specific trendy behaviors), typically lead to less stable segments.

For instance, some segmentation work done at least thirty years ago on basic social needs filled by alcoholic beverages still holds surprisingly well today. At the other extreme, segmentation done on acceptable behavior among teens five years ago would be largely useless now.

The volatility of the marketplace

Changes in number of competitors, competitive activities, or product-related technologies likely will disturb the stability of segments, and increase the likelihood of switching among segments. Indeed, the entry of any significant new competitor can have serious effects on the nature of segments.

Changes in "environmental" characteristics

Changes in various "environmental" conditions (political, legal, cultural, economic, etc.) can alter consumers' circumstances, and so can cause segments to shift. Strong external shocks to the social system can change consumer characteristics in a brief time. For instance, increased job losses and job insecurity accompanied poor-to-indifferent economic conditions between 1990 and 1991 and in downswings since. These in turn caused strong shifts in many groups' buying behavior.

Product-related seasonal patterns

Segments may hold in peak purchase months for highly seasonal products, but not otherwise. Since most purchases get made in peak months, you will want segmentation to reflect these patterns (unless you are studying the behavior in the "slow months" specifically). You would not, for instance, attempt to segment the beer market, based upon the way most users feel about the products in January. Unless you have a secret plan to change the nature of the marketplace, reaching respondents in their heavy-use months for strongly seasonal products is crucial.

3. One method proposed for checking segment stability

One concern about segments is whether they remain roughly the same over time. The only absolutely valid method for testing this is repeating the segmentation study after some months or years have passed. Still, situations may arise where you see a need to re-run original segmentation schemes to find if they still hold, but you cannot justify doing an entire new segmentation to check this.

Some methods that do not entail replicating the entire baseline study have been used with a degree of success. One of these follows. The advantage of this procedure is that you can use a smaller sample and shorter questionnaire than in a full segmentation study. This is possible because you know how many segments you are seeking to develop and the basis questions you will use. (For more detail on sample sizes, see "How Many to Sample," section IV—H). The procedure runs as follows:

- Re-survey a sample from the original population used in your baseline study. Use exactly the same basis questions as in the original study (the other questions are not necessary for this approach), and the same survey setting.

- Re-segment this new sample using the same analytical procedures as in the original baseline study. Produce the same number of segments.

- Check to determine which of the new segments most closely aligns with each original segment, by inspecting the averages (means or medians), and distributions, of each basis variable in both the original and new segment. (That is, make sure that cluster 1 in the original study remains cluster 1 in the new study. The numbers labeling the clusters may shift even if the clusters are otherwise highly similar.)

- Look for shifts going from one study to another. Are the segments nearly the same sizes? Do they differ in basic profiles on these key basis variables?

This type of method can have some obvious pitfalls if it is all you plan to do. You will save time and money only when you run this procedure and no need for segmentation emerges. If the need for segmentation does arise, however, then the total cost of course will exceed that of the segmentation study alone.

However, this type of study could be far less expensive than a full segmentation study, It possibly could be done within a budget that would not accommodate a full study, and could provide adequate evidence for funding one in the next fiscal year.

Doing this kind of study at regular intervals can help uncover unexpected shifts in the marketplace. This can work most smoothly if you set some number of differences that you will accept in advance, as a guideline for doing new segmentation. (That is, if you observe changes at some threshold greater than the one you defined, then argue to perform a new segmentation.)

We cannot overstress the importance of making sure that the basic sample frame and sample composition are precisely the same from one wave to another. It is not enough to do two years' worth of Web surveys, for instance, trusting that with basic screening in place, all will be identical. If you must have a certain level of geographic coverage, for instance, interviews from all 50 states, you need to specify this precisely when you set up the study. Too often, an interviewing service will fill a sample as you ask for it and inquire about nothing else—so you may get expectant mothers, for instance, and even if there are thousands, you may find that they do represent your intended audience geographically or by size of city, and so on.

G. Investigating Segment Homogeneity

1. The elusive concept of similarity

Homogeneity refers to the extent to which clusters cohere or hang together. It is sometimes called **intra-segment** or **within-segment homogeneity**. When you measure the homogeneity of a segment or cluster, you try to measure how well the basis variables have grouped similar individuals into that segment.

Questions concerning segment homogeneity apply only to the **market-driven (post hoc)** segmentation methods. These cannot logically apply to pre-determined (a priori) segments, because you have defined how to separate such segments in advance.

Although we intuitively understand **similarity,** mathematically the concept has proven difficult to define. Many definitions exist, but none has yet prevailed. Similarly, no definition of dissimilarity has won. Obviously, this makes it impossible to measure homogeneity in a definitive way.

Similarity measures provide some sense of the average **coherence,** or tightness of segments. Unfortunately, they give little idea of what the segments might look like, where they lie closest to each other or overlap, and their general "shape" or form.

Even if we could look at clusters in many-dimensional space (with one dimension representing each basis variable), we might not be able to "see" these patterns. Individuals would have locations in each **dimension** that reflected their responses to that question. We perhaps could identify groups of respondents with similar locations on all the dimensions. Of course, the patterns we saw would be subjective, not mathematically defined.

Unfortunately, showing and interpreting clusters graphically can prove quite difficult. Just representing three dimensions, on a sheet of two-dimensional paper, poses problems. We will see later (in section K-3) that dealing with more than two dimensions can leave many audiences quite puzzled.

All of these concerns work against our knowing definitely if clusters are good or bad in form. We would like clusters to be tightly defined, and easy to distinguish, using the variables that form the basis for clustering. However, we rarely approach perfection in actual market surveys. Sometimes just plotting the segments on two variables (or on two dimensions combining sets of variables) can show that clusters diverge greatly from the theoretical ideal, as we see in Figure 4.

2. Optimum homogeneity

The ideal would be to have completely homogeneous segments. However, this is clearly impossible; segment homogeneity will never reach an **optimum** except in theoretical exercises. You cannot get a true optimum in homogeneity unless all respondents in a segment respond identically to all basis questions.

The homogeneity of each segment almost always increases as the number of segments increases. Therefore, homogeneity is usually limited by the largest number of segments with which you **and** your audience (such as the key stakeholders) can deal effectively.

The problem you face usually is not finding the most homogeneous solution. Rather, you need to decide how much or how little homogeneity you can live with. You need to look at other criteria, some mathematical and some not.

First you must see if adding a new segment has led to any segments too small to analyze. Perhaps most importantly, though, you must determine whether the groups make more sense when you divide them more finely. As a reminder, there are almost no situations in which it makes sense to market to all segments you find. More segments therefore usually will lead to more groups that you will not include among your targets. Realistically, most organizations cannot address more than a primary and secondary target, even if their initial plans are more ambitious. So going from (say) seven to nine groups may serve no real purpose.

In considering what to choose, here as elsewhere, we will see the importance of using multiple means to evaluate the solution. You should of course examine the basic statistical tests—such as significance of group separation either by a statistical test such as overall F-values. Generally, a solution with many small clusters will show a lower set of F-values than one with larger groups.

Also, if possible, you can look into how well separated the groups are from each other when plotted in **two-dimensional space**, as we have done in figure 4 (with real clusters at the left). Procedures like discriminant analysis, discussed in section IV part I, can create this type of display. The dimensions can represent scores on a pair of variables (one for vertical and one horizontal), or can be made up of combinations of variables—but we will discuss the details of how this happens later in that section.

Real clusters typically have somewhat varying shapes and sizes when plotted, so a solution like the one to the left actually turns out to be quite good—even if not the textbook ideal. Real clusters tend to have some overlap—typically some respondents are hard to place squarely in one group.

Because small clusters often show great homogeneity, you may possibly gain insights by examining some solutions with small clusters in them. At times, these finer structures may reveal factors driving the clustering solution you have chosen.

For instance, in a study of apparel, we found a very small group that is extremely fashion conscious. Understanding the attitudes, behaviors and opinions of this splinter group helped reveal patterns in the behavior and opinions of a larger group that included many of those individuals.

Figure 4: Real-world versus theoretical clusters

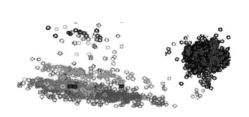

Real world clusters   Theoretical clusters

H. Segmentation Methods and Their Optimization Criteria

Each segmentation algorithm seeks to form clusters by applying some **optimization** rule. That is, the algorithm will conclude it has developed clusters when it satisfies certain mathematical criteria. These include:

- Minimization of unexplained variance (or maximizing explained variance),

- Minimization of **stress**,

- Maximization of multivariate F values,

- Maximization of a Chi-square statistic

- Maximization of cluster separation

- Getting the best **information score**.

Some segmentation models use multiple criteria. Most criteria have some relationship, but not an exact correspondence, with segment homogeneity. That is, each only refers to a certain aspect (or aspects) of the concept of **similarity.**

In addition, some methods also look at dissimilarity between clusters or at the separation of clusters. The intent of these would be to maximize the dissimilarity of individuals in different clusters.

Therefore, satisfying an **optimization criterion** of some type does not mean the cluster will be as homogenous as possible. Even if one criterion evaluates the cluster as optimally homogeneous, another criterion may not.

In addition, the clustering solution can look surprisingly different depending upon the criterion (or criteria) used. At times, these differences are subtle, and sometimes drastic, even among methods that are closely related. Later sections will discuss the tendencies of some more common methods.

However, and most importantly, none of these criteria demonstrably perform better than the others in all real-life situations. Indeed, no one method so far discovered is guaranteed to find the best solution in all situations.

Papers come out regularly proclaiming that some new method is the best, but even the most thorough paper can examine only a very small fraction of possible cases. In many instances, unfortunately, a brief reading of the paper in question will show that it is based on an unreasonably small number of variables or cases. Methods often do not scale up from simple applications to complex (and at times messy) situations.

The best policy is no doubt to keep an open mind and examine more than one solution to ensure getting the best results that you can. This will at least address the nagging question of whether you could have done better with the data.

I. Dealing with a Difficult to Segment Market

Not that many years ago, even if this was not frequent, some attempts at segmentation would end with the conclusion that the market just could not be segmented. At times, this was due to technical limitations, in particular the relatively few truly different methods for forming distinctive groups.

In a few instances, the structure of the market also might defeat attempts at segmentation. Young, Ott and Feigin (1978) identified several situations in which even trying to segment a market might prove impractical. These are the cases when undertaking a study would not be advisable.

1. **The market is too small to segment**
   Although this may seem self-evident, it is possible to underestimate the size of a marketplace until you investigate fully. For instance, a company might have a highly profitable business selling a certain type of insurance policy, and may not realize until the time of the study that only a few hundred individuals actually own that specific policy. In such a case, contemplating a segmentation study does indeed sharpen one's focus on the nature of the marketplace, but the study itself would not be feasible.

2. **Heavy users make up so large a portion of the market that it is not worth pursuing other groups**
   Most markets do indeed follow a rule similar to the well-known "80/20" rule, in which something like 80% of all business comes from something like 20% of customers. However, in the instance where a small group accounts for nearly all the volume, it would make more sense to gather as much information as possible about these individuals or organizations, rather than trying to divide up the remaining users who account for very little volume.

3. **The brand is dominant in its market**
   In spite of our government's well-intended efforts to the contrary, sometimes a brand does come to dominate its market thoroughly. In these instances, all that you need to do is develop a thorough understanding of the brand's users.

If your market does not meet any of these criteria and it proves difficult to segment, in most cases, this will be due to a lack of category-related behaviors among the basis variables. **Attitudinal segmentation**, which often did not include product-related behavior in the basis variables, seemed particularly prone to this type of failure. We should add here that this assertion will not meet with universal agreement, as there remains substantial divergence on what constitutes the "best" set of basis variables. Since Haley (1968) proposed attitudinal segmentation back in the earliest days that segmentation was even computationally possible, many have held that this is the best way to proceed. The argument goes that if groups feel differently about themselves and the world around them, then some of them would make better "target" audiences than others.

However, experience has shown that these ideas did not always survive contact with the realities of the marketplace. Even skilled practitioners could come up with groups that simply held different opinions.

In fact, the one best way to ensure that you will get a useful segmentation solution is to include category-related behaviors among the basis variables.

J. Validity: Some Approaches to This Unresolved Question

As mentioned before, the true **validity** of market segments can never be fully proven. Some methods have been used to approach the question of segment validity. However, these seldom get done in practical applications. This is usually due to costs and pressures of time. Below are some ways in which you might approach the question of validity.

- In some segmentation studies, you can test **internal validity.** For instance, for many categories, you would expect the highest rated brands on a set of attribute scales to get purchased most often. (Where highly-rated items cost much more than others in the category, however, this might not hold.)

- You could conduct controlled tests of variations in the marketing mix on small samples of each segment. Doing this, you could determine whether the segments' responses follow patterns predicted by the segmentation study. (Again, if the approach seems to work, this does not prove you have found the best possible answer.)

- Assuming you can find experts with applicable experience, you could submit the proposed segmentation to them, for their judgments on whether the proposed segments make sense.

Unfortunately none of these actually demonstrates that results will be **valid**. You might do as well to take a hard look at the results and consider whether pursuing these segments would merit a good portion of the marketing budget for the next year. If you cannot answer "yes" firmly and definitely, re-evaluate your solution. Also, think hard about whether results will look convincing to senior management. Given earlier reminders about the need to get key stakeholders involved, this seems like a minimal requirement.

Certainly, without backing from those managing the organization, the segmentation will not get any use.

In practice, trying to measure validity by estimating market shares will rarely if ever work. If your segmentation is original, shares by definition cannot be found on a segment-by-segment basis in any outside source.

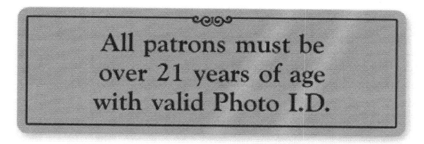

Unfortunately, for us, "validity" is not so easy to define

K. Designing Data Collection Instruments: Cost Considerations

A wide variety of considerations can influence the cost of a segmentation study. Perhaps the single area most often overlooked is the cost of internal staff time. In many cases, this does not get balanced against the cost using an outside consultant or processor for part of the study. In others, the amount of staff time needed for certain aspects of the study gets grossly underestimated.

In particular, if your staff does not have solid experience in any of the functional areas discussed, they will likely take a great deal of time, and be subject to a great deal of error.

This list describes the main areas requiring consideration in developing true costs for a segmentation study.

Problem definition:
- ⇒ Time to secure senior management's involvement,
- ⇒ Any interviews with stakeholders or other internal audiences
- ⇒ Estimating the research staff's time and effort,
- ⇒ Any required pre-study qualitative research,
- ⇒ Any outside consulting (for instance, about approaches and algorithms).

Research design:
- ⇒ Using staff vs. outside suppliers to design and perform the study,
- ⇒ Sample design—making sure you have enough for the intended uses,
- ⇒ Steps needed to develop the survey instrument.

Data collection:
- ⇒ Interview method,
- ⇒ Interview length,
- ⇒ Interview recruitment procedures,
- ⇒ Any requirements for incentives
- ⇒ Incidence of target population,
- ⇒ Supervision requirements,
- ⇒ Editing and coding.

Data analysis:
- ⇒ Segment determination,
- ⇒ Segment profiling,
- ⇒ Modeling or simulation
- ⇒ Development of scoring tools for use in later studies
- ⇒ Post-segmentation in-depth interviewing or "ethnographic" investigations.

({Portions adapted from Neal, 1990)

L. The Basic Segmentation Issues (Recap)

☑ Segmentation represents a basic difference in approach from econometric models and from product differentiation.

☑ You perform segmentation because you expect to find differences in response to your marketing efforts among the various segments.

☑ Groups that do not differ in behavior are not segments, just groups. Many structures other than segments exist in markets.

☑ You must be able to identify segments, reach them and appeal to them selectively.

☑ Strong differences exist between the two basic approaches to segmentation: Predetermined (a priori) vs. market-driven (post-hoc).

☑ Selecting the basis variables constitutes a crucial decision in segmentation.

☑ Descriptive variables build understanding of segments and allow you to reach them selectively..

☑ Probability samples among a given audience are a needed for projecting segmentation results.

☑ Data reliability more often gets mentioned than acted upon in segmentation.

☑ Segment stability has three aspects to consider: time, situation, and season.

☑ Optimal segment homogeneity is an important issue, about which we still have no definitive answers.

☑ The question of validity also remains open. True validity is an elusive goal.

☑ Recall also that validity often gets confused with validation.

☑ Management must support and remain involved in segmentation.

☑ Many issues likely will affect costs; internal staff time most often gets forgotten.

IV. TECHNICAL ASPECTS OF SEGMENTATION: DATA COLLECTION AND ANALYSIS

A. Preparing Clean Data

B. Conditioning the Data

C. Detail on Methods for Segmentation: Cluster Analysis

D. Automatic Interaction Detection (A.I.D.) and CHAID

E. Using Correspondence Analysis in Clustering

F. Uses of Factor Analysis in Clustering

G. Conjoint, Choice or MaxDiff Utilities as the Basis for Clustering

H. How Many to Sample

I. Using Discriminant Analysis to Extend Clustering Analysis

J. Selecting the Number of Segments

K. Profiling and Locating the Segments

L. Classification Tree Models for Respondent Profiling

M. Descriptive Profiling

N. Fuzzy Classification

O. Q-Factor Analysis: A discredited Approach

P. When Segmentation Produces Poor Results

Q. Putting the Results to Work

R. In Conclusion

A. Preparing Clean Data

1. Overview: a critical process

Issues in preparing **clean data** are much the same in segmentation research as in any research. However, these concerns take on even more importance in segmentation, because many of the procedures are extremely sensitive to anomalies in the data. Manual data entry is quickly fading as a practice, but cleaning data remains critical if respondents are providing answers on the Web.

Data entry, or what gets into the survey, often represents a major source of error in market research. Two principal issues arise in the control of data entry errors:

- Trusting to the Web vs. watching everything

  The Web provides a wonderful world of convenience. Even if we must phone people to locate them (as with low incidence professional populations), data may still get entered via PC or device. Since we rarely use paper questionnaires, a whole host of issues related to **data cleaning** have largely vanished. Data, though, still must get cleaned in some way if you are using open-ended questions, and to check for inconsistency. The content of open-ended questions in Web surveys that people fill in themselves usually leaves much to be desired. And if those responses go into text analysis, somebody will need to clean them to remove the many extraneous and unintelligible comments. You can take things as they come, but odds of this being productive are low.

- Using inside resources vs. an outside contractor

  With some open ended responses or in the rare instance of having to use paper questionnaires, you must do something to enter the data. This looks easy until you try to get staff members to do it. Even people very skilled at the keyboard or on a device will find data entry difficult if they have no training in it. Unless you are a very unusual organization with a seasoned data entry group, this one job is better left to experienced outsiders.

  Data cleaning involves testing and editing individual responses for internal consistency and assuring that instructions, such as skip patterns, were followed correctly. Cleaning, as noted, remains as important as ever now that we ask respondents to fill in Web surveys—or worse, supply answers on some mobile device. Several issues arise in data cleaning:

- **Look-up** cleaning vs. **forced** cleaning

  Forced data cleaning happens when strange-seeming answers automatically get replaced or removed from all respondents' responses. For instance, a respondent who said she used a product would get her earlier response on product awareness **forced** to "yes," even if she did not answer that question.

  This type of cleaning can introduce problems, especially if you do not know that it is being done. In the example above, it could be possible for a respondent to use certain products, and to remember them **only** in the context of this use. Forcing what seems logical into the data may introduce inaccuracies in such cases.

  In other cases, forcing is the best thing and yet may not get done. For instance, a respondent may say in an initial usage question that they do not use the product. Later questions involve purchasing the product for different occasions, but they get skipped for the respondent, rather than filled with the available "never do this" code. Clearly, this could be argued, but then and again, when one never does something with a product filling in this way just might correspond to reality.

2. Specific concerns in editing, coding and cleaning: identifying acceptable questionnaires

Again, as important as these are in any study, problems in any of these areas can actually cause fatal damage in a segmentation study. This is so because of the sensitivity of many clustering methods to anomalies (in particular extreme values) and to subtle patterns in the data. For instance, **mean filling** (substituting the mean or average response for a blank) could actually create a segment strongly influenced by these filled values. Some considerations in whether a questionnaire meets an acceptable level follow below:

- Proportion answered (minimum acceptable level of refused/no answer responses),

- quality of responses (apparent comprehension of questions and effort in answers),

- response patterns to scaled items (any apparent randomness in responses, tendency to use only one or two points on scales, etc.),

- signs in the responses of an inappropriate respondent (actually out of age quota, wrong household composition or product use patterns, etc.),

- acceptability of an incomplete questionnaire,

- timing of the interview vs. the average.

Taking these into account, you may then need to decide how to handle any **outliers** (anomalous-seeming respondents).

In addition, these are some minimal checks in editing. Make sure that those editing inspect:

- Legibility/intelligibility of recorded responses,

- completeness, accuracy, and consistency,

- whether skip patterns were followed.

Coding should also follow, at a minimum, several basic rules:

- using mutually exclusive and collectively exhaustive codes,

- retaining as much coding detail as possible (better to trim more detail than to omit detail in the first pass),

- using consistent codes for missing values (for example, consistently 9, or 99)

- assuming you want to manually divide continuous variables, such as percentages, for use (e.g.) in cross-tabulation, choosing consistent "break points," to ensure across-question comparability.

The issues of respondents cheating and responding randomly on the Web loom large, and indeed dealing with these can take considerable expertise. Cheating means people responding to a survey where they are not qualified—or more than once to a survey. For certain topics, cheating can be detected by questions that require true expertise in the area. Duplicate responses are often caught because the person returns to the same PC to respond more than once and so has the same IP address, but two user names. Many vendors now routinely look at IP addresses—but it always pays to check.

Catching random responses requires particular attention to two issues. First, what consti-tutes **speeding** through a survey. and second, which patterns of responses look suspi-ciously too uniform or **straight line**.

(Portions adapted from Sonquist & Dunkelburg, 1977).

3. Other considerations: missing data and data weighting

Missing data problems

This is a leading problem in preparing data for multivariate analysis. Many multivariate procedures cannot handle missing data, leading to either:

- **case-wise** deletion, or
- **list-wise** deletion of respondents.

When list-wise deletion is done, a respondent with one missing response will get dropped entirely from the analysis. Case-wise deletion does not drop respondents for one missing response, but it is inconsistent to the extent that many statisticians call it "unwise" deletion.

Many methods for trying to avoid this (for filling the blanks) have been developed. Common among these are the following:

- Mean substitution (replacing a blank with the mean value for that variable),
- median substitution,
- substitution of the mid-point or end-point of a scale.

Newer methods, such as EM and Bayesian imputation tend to perform better. Both look at patterns in the respondent's other responses and the responses of other respondents, although in different ways. Using either will tend to preserve the overall mean value, but typically will decrease the overall variance or variability of responses. (They are, after all filling in "average" values based on sophisticated criteria, and it follows logically that more averages will decrease variability.) These can work quite well with a limited percentage of missing responses.

However, no method of adjustment performs in an entirely satisfactory way. The problem is that whenever you **fill** an answer, you provide data the respondents did not. This can introduce major distortions if you have a high level of missing values.

As an added caution, note that some analysts (wrongly) claim they can accurately "guess" missing responses. They usually do this by applying differences from other questions actually answered and using these to fill in the blanks. That is, they subtract some arbitrary value from the response to another question, and put this into the blank space. This type of approach has no place in multivariate analysis.

Another (this time legitimate) approach involves developing **imputed** responses, based on reducing variance in some dependent variable. The CHAID technique can do this. (Section IV - B.5 will discuss this in more depth.)

Differential weighting of data

Try to avoid weighting data in any way before doing segmentation. Weighting data before you develop segments can introduce anomalies. Segments may appear (or disappear) simply because certain respondents have extra weight. Some newer segmentation routines (e.g., TwoStep in SPSS) even will turn off weighting automatically before they run.

B. Conditioning Data: Standardizing is Important

Standardizing variables before subjecting them to any clustering procedure almost always makes sense. This is so because differences in the scales of variables can influence the results from many clustering procedures.

Most of the larger statistics packages (SPSS, Systat, SAS, BMDP, etc.) provide standardization among their built-in data transformations. These transformation procedures are quick and relatively painless to use.

Standardization, as a reminder, means transforming all variables to a common scale. In this scale, each variable has a mean of zero and a standard deviation of 1. This will remove the effects that can arise solely from differences in the scales of variables.

Two instances arise in which not to standardize:

1. In studies using volumetric data where the purpose of clustering is to form groups differentiated by volume usage profiles. (Of course, all the volume measures should use the same scale.)
2. In studies clustering on **conjoint analysis utilities**. If these are the sole ingredient among the basis variables, it is not appropriate to standardize these utilities because range differences in conjoint utilities show differences in variables' importance.

However, conjoint analysis and discrete choice modeling **(DCM)**—although both methods that trade off multiple attributes—require different treatment. We discuss these further in section IV-G. If these terms are completely unfamiliar, please see the brief explanations there.

Discrete choice modeling can produce individual-level utilities, but doing so requires that the analysis use **Hierarchical Bayesian** (HB) methods. Another method we will discuss, Maximum Difference (MaxDiff) scaling also can be analyzed in this way. HB methods may be familiar to some readers, but for the rest it may suffice to say that the process is highly complex and computer-intensive.

The utilities produced by this type of analysis will vary in scale somewhat from respondent to respondent—so everything done with these utilities must standardize them within the respondent. Most usefully, these utilities can be turned into individual-level **importances** by a process involving exponentiation and division. Once this has been done, all the utilities have a common scale—from zero to 100%. These transformed utilities then can be used in segmentation.

One interesting property of utilities, whether from conjoint analysis, MaxDiff or discrete choice modeling, is that if these make up a large proportion of the basis variables, clusters often will look like text-book examples, with clearly defined differences and little overlap.

C. Detail on Methods for Segmentation: Cluster Analysis

1. What it is

Cluster analysis includes many techniques aimed at separating (classifying) respondents or objects into groups (clusters). Groups form so that any member of a group has more similarities to other members of that group than to members of other groups.

2. Some basic principles of cluster analysis

a.   Cluster analysis can work in two basically different ways. That is, you can perform clustering either upon:

- individuals' similarities across variables (clustering them on their responses), as gets done in many segmentation studies, or,
- variables' similarities across respondents, as gets done in some positioning studies.

b.   Each object can belong to one and only one group. (**Clumping** or overlapping cluster analysis—apparently rarely used outside linguistics—does not have this assumption.)

c.   The analyst's judgment will have a major influence on the results. You will need to decide about:

- variables to enter into the clustering procedure,
- selecting weights, if any, given to the variables,
- procedures used for clustering, and
- number of clusters to generate.

We should note that some newer methods, such as TwoStep clustering, X-means clustering and latent class clustering can make recommendations about how many clusters to select. With some software, this "best" solution is presented by default.

However, even if your software does this, the mathematically best solution may not be the one that fits your needs. It may even turn out to have almost no practical value, for instance, a division into three groups such as: those consistently rating low, those who are middling raters and those who tend to rate higher. Unfortunately, some automated clustering routines seem to have some fondness for finding such solutions. Alternatively, you may find useless groupings if different respondents tend to have different styles in responding to questions.

If the software has an automated facility for selecting the solution it judges to be best, you still are best served by examining a range of solutions, rather than happily accepting the first offered. Your strategic needs, rather than the software's conception of what is best, should drive the final selection.

3. What to expect from the output

Clustering programs vary widely in the nature of their output. However, most programs are surprisingly silent about the details of the solution they have provided, beyond some summary numbers. In many cases, this will include at least one of these:

- respondent classification into a pre-specified number of groups or some maximum number of groups,

- average scores in each cluster for the variables chosen as the basis for clustering,

- a full clustering sequence (for instance a "tree diagram," or a dendrogram) for some of the methods,

- some measure of each cluster's variability or the variability of the total solution. For instance, you might see:

  - the statistical significance of differences between the groups

  - the mean or average F-ratio

  - the density of the groups (how closely members group around the cluster's **centroid** (or group average),

  - the **variance explained** by the classification,

  - the **information score** and so on.

In fact, some methods even remain mum about basics such as how many respondents ended in each group formed. As a result, you typically will have to rely on other methods to help you understand the nature of the solutions you have developed. Among these are discriminant analysis, analysis of variance, and multivariate mapping.

Later sections will address all these points in more detail.

Like most cluster output, not too informative

4. Types of cluster analysis algorithms

The various algorithms primarily cluster together individuals who respond similarly to a set of basis questions. Most clustering algorithms used in marketing and market research fall into two broad classes:

- **hierarchical** procedures,
- **iterative** (or **optimizing**) procedures.

Hierarchical methods fall into two broad classes:

- **agglomerative**, and
- **divisive**.

In **hierarchical agglomerative procedures**, each respondent starts as an individual cluster, and these clusters get aggregated (or "agglomerated") at each step, based on certain criteria. Criteria used include, for instance, reaching some minimum or maximum multivariate distance between the clusters formed.

Divisive hierarchical procedures get far less use than the agglomerative procedures. In the divisive methods, respondents start as one large cluster and split into smaller groups.

In **iterative procedures**, all respondents start in a single cluster, which gets partitioned or separated into groups. These procedures work through the initial solution several times (hence the name "iterative"). Some partitioning procedures, such as the Howard-Harris algorithm, successively partition the data set at each step, based on some criterion such as minimizing the multivariate variance, or maximizing the distance between multivariate cluster means. These procedures often can "recover" from a poor initial partitioning of the sample, because respondents can move from cluster to cluster in later partitionings.

Hierarchical methods develop only one scheme for dividing the sample. If the initial split of the sample is poor, these methods cannot recover.

Several other broad families of clustering methods exist. However, these mostly get applied in other disciplines--and in some cases, hardly at all. These methods include:

- fuzzy clustering,
- density searching methods,
- clumping procedures,
- graphical analytical methods,
- model based methods, including latent class and finite mixture (or FIMIX) clustering, and
- some newer methods, including TwoStep cluster, EM clustering, spectral clustering, latent class clustering, and indeed a whole host of others.

Fuzzy clustering does not assign any respondent entirely to a group. Rather, it gives the respondent a probability of belonging to each group. Section IV - N will discuss ways in which you can extend any clustering procedure to take on aspects of fuzzy clustering.

Model-based methods first construct a schematic of how the variables work together, then build clusters from that representation. In the case of **finite mixture models**

(FIMIX), this typically would be a complex extension of regression called a partial least squares (PLS) path model. In this, similar variables are gathered into groups (like the factors in factor analysis), and then patterns of influence are sought between these groups and some target variable—and also among the various variable groups.

It is quite an appealing idea that we might first construct a model of variables working together, and then—finding that model reasonable—use it to generate groups. However, if our analytical goal is to predict some target variable, it is unrealistic to expect that the method also will do the best in generating distinctive groupings. Sometimes, of course, differences among the groups found in this way will be dramatic, but in many cases the groups generated will be not sharply different from each other.

TwoStep and **EM clustering**, like **latent class analysis**, can group respondents using many kinds of variables, including nominal, scaled and continuous. These help expand the number of questions and concerns that can be included in clustering, However, like all methods, these do not seem to do particularly well when required to process too many different types of variables addressing many different concerns. No hard and fast rules exist for where the line between "many" and "too many" lies. This needs to be determined by trial and experience.

Clumping, spectral clustering and many graphical analytical methods, which get little use in marketing and market research, fall beyond the scope of this book.

5. Fundamental consistency problems in many clustering algorithms

Many clustering programs may provide inconsistent or unstable results. All clustering routines have certain limitations. The most commonly used clustering methods differ from nearly all multivariate procedures in that they are not guaranteed to be reliable. That is, you can re-run a clustering procedure, using the same data, and get different results each time. Therefore, thoroughly checking segments generated by clustering procedures is important.

A number of methods exist for checking for inconsistencies. Two methods are common:

⇒ Use split samples, or holdout samples, to verify the results of the initial clustering.

⇒ Use different clustering procedures and determine the extent to which the results are compatible. Checking one solution's average level of agreement with the clustering assignments from a range of other methods can help assess the strength of a solution.

That is, if the clustering assignments are more consistent with the average assignments across a number of other methods, that can be one argument in favor of a solution. A solution that is unlike all others has a strong likelihood of not being the best way to divide up people.

6. Basics about clustering routines

a. Hierarchical methods

These fall into the "agglomerative" methods and the "divisive" methods. The first, the agglomerative type, gets the most (reported) use of all types of clustering, according to several surveys of the literature. Divisive methods rarely get used.

Agglomerative methods start by identifying each respondent as a "cluster." These algorithms then seek the most similar respondent, and join these two into a cluster. They then search for the next closest respondent, link this respondent to first two, and so on. The procedure forms a so-called "tree diagram." A small tree diagram, linking 8 respondents, follows.

Figure 5: Clusters formed by a hierarchical method

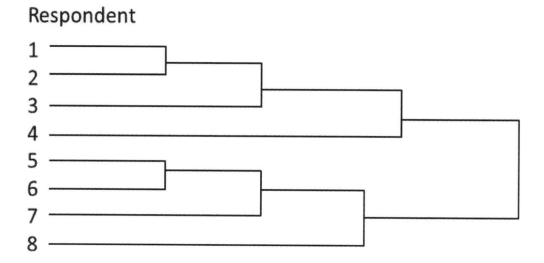

The diagram provides a "road map" for the way the clusters will form. This chart shows the similarity of respondents by how close (to the left) their "branches" in the tree join. Respondents for whom this left-to-right distance is largest would be most dissimilar. Note that each small cluster gets included along with one or more others to form a larger cluster. These larger clusters in turn get combined. Finally, all respondents become one large cluster.

In the diagram above, we can see two larger clusters, the first formed by respondents 1 to 4, and the second by respondents 5 to 8. In the first of these clusters, respondents 1 and 4 are most dissimilar. In the second, respondents 5 and 8 are most dissimilar.

In divisive clustering, all respondents start as one large cluster, and move to smaller and smaller groups. You would get a similar tree diagram, but would read it from right to left.

b. Hierarchical agglomerative methods

These methods fall into several classes, with a wealth of names used for each. These names can refer to a specific type of clustering, or even to specific algorithms. These get mixed and matched with some abandon, even by relatively informed writers on the subject. As a result, classifications remain unclear.

To make matters less clear, not all authors agree on where various procedures belong. For instance, at least one writer (W. Neal) classifies **Ward's method** with **variance-reducing** optimizing methods, while many others say it belongs with the **linkage methods**, even though it links groups by a process of variance reduction. (Details on optimizing methods will follow.)

These are the broad classes of methods and some of the terminology you may encounter:

- **Single linkage methods**
  - Names include: minimum method, nearest neighbor method, connectiveness method.

- **Complete linkage methods**
  - Names include: maximum method, furthest neighbor, diameter method.

- **Average linkage methods**
  - Names include: weighted average method, median method, centroid method, Gower's method.

- **Variance reduction methods**
  - Names include: Ward's method most commonly; others mentioned include HGroup, ESS method, CLUSTAN (in part; this has other methods in it). Also, you may encounter a method SPAD. This used to be mainly a clustering method, but in more recent years appears to have grown into an entire data analytic suite. It can work with non-metric data, by including output from the Benzecri method of correspondence analysis.

These methods usually more computer time and memory than the iterative methods we discuss next. This is much less a concern now than it was not that many years ago. Older books on clustering may warn about using these methods with more than 200 to 250 cases. These constraints are no longer a concern.

Clustering by hierarchical methods using cases counting in the tens or hundreds of thousands of cases—and more—has become easily possible. There may be a small but discernible difference in processing time with extremely large samples—this family of methods tends to run somewhat more slowly than the iterative ones (described in the next section).

c. Iterative (or optimization) methods

These seek to find "optimal" combinations of respondents based on several different criteria. Perhaps most commonly used is the K-Means type of procedure, under one of its many names.

These start by dividing or partitioning the sample, in some preliminary way, into the number of clusters you specify. They then try to move from this "initial partitioning" to an "optimum" solution.

These procedures usually permit cluster members to "cross over" between clusters at each partitioning step, and so allow for some recovery from a poor initial partitioning. (There remains some debate about how well some of these procedures, in particular the K-Means method, can recover from an extremely poor initial partition.)

Again, many names have been applied to the various clustering routines. These are some varieties of partitioning algorithms:
- K - Means (e.g., Howard-Harris, Forgy, BCTRY, Carmone's, reflected or Jancey, etc.),
- K-Means as defined by SAS (FASTCLUS), SPSS, also the other major packages such as Systat, Statistica, Stata,
- Wolfe's Method,
- Hill climbing algorithms,
- Combined hill-climbing & K-Means (CLUS, MIKCA).

Differences between these alternative methods can be subtle. The ways in which each works best remains in some dispute.
One pitfall associated with all optimizing methods is hitting upon a **local maximum,** or not truly optimal solution. This can happen because the number of possible partitions becomes astronomical even in a modestly-sized sample. Therefore, various shortcuts (or **heuristics**) that try to approximate the "optimum" have been devised. One or more of these will get applied in some way in each algorithm.

Any of these methods can be used with **seeding**. This uses a small sample (say 100) divided by one of the hierarchical methods, which gives a set of **initial group centers** or **seeds.** These are then used as the starting points around which the final clusters coalesce. Because the starting points come from an actual clustering—even with a small sample— these often can reach a good final solution. The default iterative clustering methods in statistics packages often start building groups from extreme values or completely random values—and so may never reach a good solution.

Some procedures, like seeding, seem to deal well with real-world data in many instances. However, trying to find the true "optimal solution" remains problematic. This has been compared to a person parachuting to a patch of hilly ground, blindfolded, and then trying to find the highest point. Unfortunately, even in testing how well the procedure has done, you may have little more luck than the blindfolded parachutist.

7. Which method works best?

All clustering procedures share one basic problem. While they are **pattern-seeking** proce-dures, all algorithms, to a greater or lesser extent, **impose patterns**.

Among the hierarchical methods, the single linkage approaches tend to produce long "chain -like" structures. As a result, it can combine dissimilar respondents into large groups.

In studies with data of a known form, Ward's and the complete linkage method sometimes failed when the data formed elongated ("ellipsoid") or odd-shaped clusters (as charted on a two dimensional chart using the key basis variables as the axes.) These methods tend to pro-duce small spherical clusters. At least one study showed Ward's also to do poorly with clus-ters known to have unequal diameters.

Some authors have put average linkage methods forward as avoiding the extremes of either of the other linkage methods. However, these methods may do poorly when clusters are not clearly separated.

Among the iterative (optimizing) partitioning methods, the K-Means approach tends to find "hyper-spherical," highly homogeneous clusters. These methods are particularly sensitive to changes in the scale of the data. Standardization of data can help this approach avoid some problems with differences in variables' scales.

The "hill-climbing" methods can sometimes create clusters of nearly equal size, whether or not these are present in the data.

Newer methods, such as SPSS TwoStep and latent classes can sometimes find clusters of mixed shapes in one data set. However, no studies to date show clearly where either of these methods, or indeed other newer methods (such as EM and spectral clustering) tend to do best or worst.

Some authors say that certain algorithms seem more appropriate for marketing research than others. For instance, Neal (1989) finds the single linkage methods least useful because of their tendencies to "chain" data and to develop large non-homogenous clusters. Over many years, in most studies where clustering methods try to restore data with known structures, single linkage has had the least success (Kaufmann and Rousseeuw, 1990).

The idea of locating tight, spherical clusters seems to agree intuitively--at least in part--with "targeting" relatively well-defined segments. However, this makes sense only if the proce-dure does not force this shape onto the data.

Unfortunately, we cannot look into a high-dimensional space, simultaneously seeing how responses scatter on many questions. Portraying even three dimensions on paper becomes quite difficult. The question of a "best" method seems likely to remain open. For now, we can-not do better than taking into account the limitations of each method as we examine the solution it generates.

Not yet awarded to any clustering method

D. Classification Trees (CHAID, CRT, and Related Methods)

1. Basics/objectives

Classification tree or CHAID- and CRT-related procedures split a sample into non-overlapping subgroups, to maximize between-group differences on some dependent variable. We can include such closely related procedures as CRT (or C&RT or CART) in this discussion, although they have some differences in how they behave.

The target variable could be buying intentions, overall ratings, or product use level. These procedures allow you to analyze data with no **ordinal** or **interval** value—along with scales and measurements in the same analysis. For instance, they can process **categorical** variables like regions of the country, where, for instance, a code "5" does not have 5 times the numeric worth of a code "1." These procedures therefore can do many things most multivariate procedures cannot. One more popular variant is called CHAID (or chi-squared AID). It has salient advantages over the long-departed traditional AID, as section D-3 below will discuss. The remainder of this section refers to the CHAID procedure. CRT is similar but handles continuous variables differently and has less flexibility in how it splits variables.

A distinctive feature of CHAID is that it provides **situational** or **conditional** probabilities. That is, it looks for values of one variable that have predictive value conditional on the values of some other variables or variables. This "nesting" of variables makes the procedure particularly useful in seeking high incidences of a given group. This may sound abstract, but the example following should clear up what happens.

An example of CHAID in action

Let's suppose you wanted to find out what most distinguishes light from medium from heavy users of a product, based on responses to 80 question items, including demographics. This fictional example appears on the sample tree diagram on the next page. You may wish to refer to this diagram along with the description.

CHAID would first split the sample on the one variable producing the greatest between-group differences. Suppose this is respondent's age group. Looking just at the heavy users, you would then see that they make up:

- 20% of the sample overall,
- 8% of the 18-24 age group,
- 11% of the 25-34, and
- 36% of the 35-54 group.

Also, CHAID formed this last group by combining two groups, those ages 35-44 and those ages 45-54.

The procedure would then continue within each group devised in the last step. Looking just at the 35-54 age group, you might find that region of the country best differentiated among light, medium, and heavy users. Here, you find that region 3 (Midwest) has the highest incidence of heavy users within the 35-54 year age group (56%), while region 4 (South) has the lowest incidence (23%). The procedure here combined regions 2 and 4 (East and West) into one group. The level of incidence of heavy users in this group was 34%.

Note that the very high incidence group just uncovered must **first** be age 35-54 and next live in the Midwest. This is an example of a conditional probability.

2. CHAID output: a section of a tree diagram

This is just a small section of a tree, shown to highlight how they work. A full tree likely would have splits below the other age groups and even within the regions that appear in the third row (or tier) down. Crucial to the output of CHAID is a tree structure that shows, at each stage:

- The independent variable best dividing the sample, and how that variable is split,
- The number of individuals "split off" into each of the groups,
- Key dependent-variable values among each of the groups split off (for example, the percentage of heavy users in each subgroup),
- The number in each "node," or splitting point.

Figure 6: A section of a CHAID classification tree

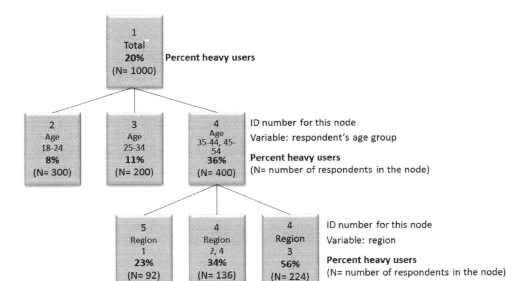

Trees can display other information as well, or suppress some of the detail shown above. A table giving a complete breakdown, showing the incidence of all groups at each point in this diagram, may follow.

When this table is shown in order of incidence, starting with the highest incidence group, it is called a "Gains Chart" or a "Leverage Chart." This chart can provide a highly valuable summary of the tree and has direct applications for marketing, as will be discussed in the section on profiling segments. Overall, CHAID, CRT and related procedures have the most value in profiling and do not perform particularly well in creating segments. The groups formed tend to be too small to serve as useful targets.

Some CHAID-related programs also can produce highly detailed summaries of every step in its analysis. These show how the sample split, best and other significant predictors at each point, and so on. These do not get much use, though, as a complete CHAID history can cover hundreds of pages.

3. CHAID versus traditional A.I.D.

CHAID (Chi-squared A.I.D.), is an extension of the much older and more basic Automatic Interaction Detection (or AID). Many variants of CHAID exist as well, some that you may encounter including C4.5, C5.0 and J48. Any CHAID-based procedure represents a significant advance over traditional A.I.D.. Although once popular, traditional A.I.D. has fallen by the wayside today because of its relative shortcomings.

The earliest form of A.I.D. did not adjust significance testing for the number of possible ways a sample could be split. This had the effect of allowing variables with more distinct values to "explain" more variance than those with fewer. Therefore, the variables with more values or codes would "float to the top," and appear as the best explanatory variables. This was a salient problem. There simply are more ways to divide a sample if you have more codes to work with—and so you have more chances of "finding" some significant difference.

The real breakthrough in CHAID came from better statistical testing, tailoring test thresholds to the number of comparisons is very precise ways. At the time, this was considered advanced enough to get reported in a symposium on artificial intelligence.

CHAID also can perform "optimal recoding" of independent variables, which is grouping or rearranging codes to maximize separation of the groups formed. That is, on a 10-point scale, for instance, CHAID might split the predictor into 1 through6, 7 and 8, 9 only and 10 only if that was the sharpest contrast. Doing this can involve checking thousands of possible ways of dividing the variable. In addition, CHAID can assign "don't know" responses to the group (or groups) which will maximize this separation.

4. Limitations of CHAID

While CHAID was designed to process non-metric and non-ordinal data that normal multivariate analyses cannot handle, it has certain limitations:

- Predictors *must* be ordinal, nominal or interval, and *not metric*. CHAID will automatically "bin" continuous variables into some number of even-sized groups (or you can decide the number or do alternative custom "binning"). The number of bins will influence the significance of results—with more bins and results have a lower chance of passing as significant. The defaults for most packages seem to be either 10 or 20 "bins."
- You must specify a "response" or dependent variable—this is similar to the grouping variable in discriminant analysis. CHAID will divide the sample to maximize between-group differences on this variable. If you have no such dependent variable, CHAID will not run. You can, however, run CHAID using such dependent variables as segments generated by a clustering procedure—and we will see how powerful that can be in later sections.

5. CHAID versus more familiar multivariate procedures

CHAID searches by a sequential procedure. Therefore, you do not need to specify an explicit **effects** model as you might with, for instance, analysis of variance. Unlike nearly all multivariate procedures, CHAID analyzes data based on situational or conditional probabilities. This is where the term **interaction** applies. All later partitions of the sample depend on earlier ones as their starting points. The variables therefore **interact.** Finding these patterns—where variables' effects depend on other variables in complex ways—can provide uniquely valuable insights.

E. Using Correspondence Analysis in Clustering

Correspondence analysis most often gets used in segmentation to create compelling graphical displays that portray the similarities and differences among clusters. In these displays, each cluster appears as a point, and each attribute scored by the clusters appears as another point. Points for the attributes fall closest to the clusters where their scores are highest. Clusters that are similar to each other fall close to each other. Finally attributes that are rated most similarly across clusters tend to fall near each other. This is shown in Figure 6 at the bottom.

More rarely, correspondence can be used in clustering. This can be done because this multivariate procedure develops "internal scales" for a set of variables. These scales resemble the principal components generated by factor analysis, (both come from "decomposing" a matrix, a process of trying to capture most of the information in a reduced set of rows and columns). However, correspondence analysis, unlike factor analysis, can scale nominal variables into metric measures.

That is, this method develops multivariate **spaces** and each respondent has **loadings**, or metric values, in this space. These loadings for individuals then could form the basis for clustering. This works much like clustering with principal component scores developed by factor analysis. The result: clustering of cases based on the similarities in their locations, in the space defined by the correspondence analysis. However, these spaces, like factors, could prove difficult to cluster. We will discuss this problem in Section F, following this.

Most statistical software does not cluster directly based on correspondence analysis. One program that does is called "SPAD." SPAD has grown quite a bit over the years and now includes a wide range of procedures. It is called a data mining tool by at least one Web site.

Figure 7: Correspondence map of segments and attributes most strongly related to them

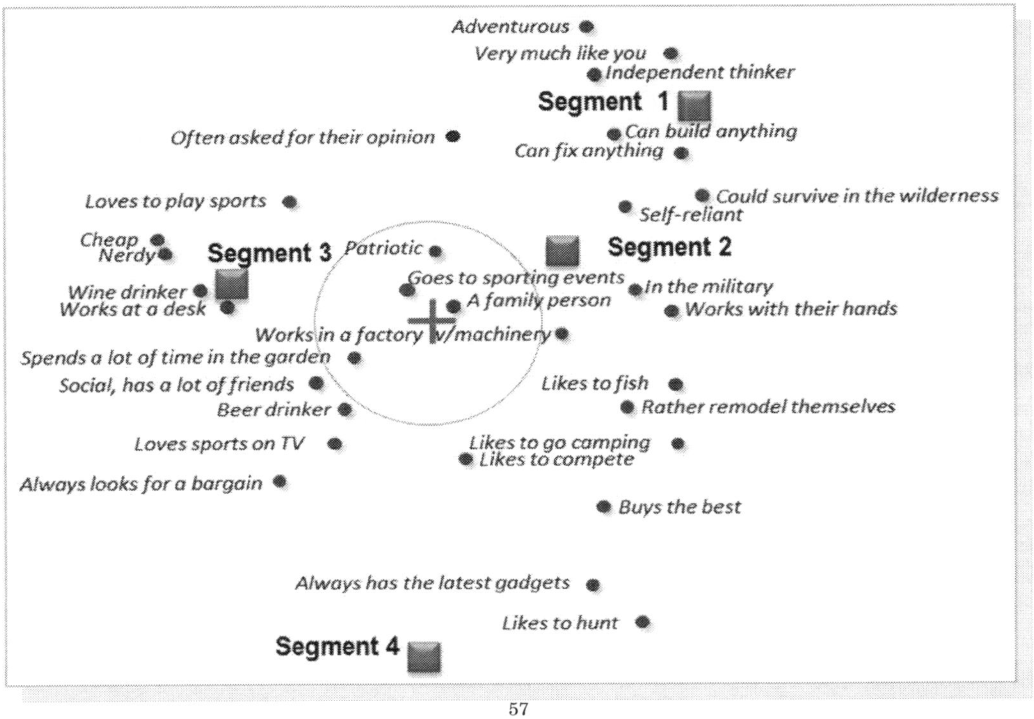

F. The Use of Factor Scores in a Clustering Procedure

1. Basics

Where the researcher faces large numbers of basis variables, or finds high levels of correlation between the basis variables, a factor analysis (or the closely-related principal components analysis) can help make the data set more manageable.

As a reminder, the basic aim of factor analysis is to take many variables, and reduce these to a smaller number of "factors." Each factor can be thought of as the basic **idea** or **theme** expressed by a group of variables.

A variable's **factor loading** can be thought of as the strength of that variable's relationship to the factor. High-loading variables have strong relationships to a given factor, low-loading ones weak relationships.

Factor analysis does not automatically generate a "correct" number of factors. You must decide, based on how much of the information in the original variables you want to keep, how much sense the factors seem to make, and the number of factors you find helpful.

2. Using factor scores versus using selected variables in clustering

Factor analysis often gets applied in this way: factor analysis produces principal component (or factor) scores, which then become the basis variables in a clustering procedure. Another, and often better, procedure is simply to use factor analysis to screen the variables. You would use the factor solution to choose about an equal number of variables from each factor. Doing this prevents you from accidentally "weighting" your solution toward one factor. This has the salient advantage of not altering the data's form—factors are composites of several or many variables, but not the original data.

- For instance, suppose you perform a factor analysis on 50 variables. You find 10 variables loading significantly into the first factor, and only 4 loading into the second. If you segmented using all these variables, your solution might over-emphasize the concern captured by first factor. Unless you knew this to reflect the outside world, the segments would simply reflect the way you constructed your questionnaire.

- You could use the results from the factor analysis to drop 4 to 6 of the variables in the first factor from your basis variables. (In most instances, you would drop some of variables with the lowest loadings.) The solution you get from cutting some variables in this way should represent the marketplace more accurately.

- Please recall **always to use a "rotation" of the factor solution** when you use factors to screen variables. Without a technical discussion, we can say rotation is a process that straightens out the allocation of variables to factors. Without rotation, we tend to get a large "everything" first factor, with many variables bunched together, and then very small ones. Rotation comes by many names—among them, the "orthogonal" ones are called such things as Varimax, Equimax and Quartimax. There also are "oblique" rotations, but these are hard to understand. They would correspond to having an x/y axis that is not at right angles. Interpretation becomes very hard with this. Fortunately, whichever "orthogonal" rotation you choose, the results will be much the same. Just pick the one that has the most appealing name, but do use one.

3. Cautions on using factor scores as a basis for clustering

As a reminder, many clustering procedures show great sensitivity to the scale and the form of the data. In particular, changes in the form of the data can produce extreme effects on the final solutions in K-Means type procedures. Using factor scores in clustering can at times lead to results differ radically from the solution based on the original data set. This can happen even when the principal components explain very high proportions of variance in the original data. (See also the discussion by Everitt [1980]). Practical experience shows that clustering on factor scores in fact may not yield results closely mirroring clustering on standardized data.

Richard Johnson (in a private communication) has suggested that factor scores can cause problems in clustering due to workings of the **central limit theorem**. In brief, this theorem says that repeated samples from a given population taken together will approximate a **normal distribution**. If you think of each question put into a factor solution as one "sample," then you would expect the sum of these samples to produce a relatively smooth normal curve. Such smooth curves can prove difficult to segment in any logical way.

For instance, a 3-dimensional (multivariate) normal distribution would look something like a watermelon. Unfortunately, no arguably best way of dividing a shape like this has been found. You could more easily see where to divide something more "gritty" or "lumpy," such as a bunch of grapes. Johnson argues that raw data has more of a gritty structure than factors. Raw data therefore lends itself better to clustering.

Informal comparisons using real-world data has usually shown the raw attributes typically produce more clearly defined cluster structures than factor scores based on the same data. In some cases, no practical difference emerged. However, in no instance have we yet observed use of factor scores to produce a more clearly defined set of clusters than the actual data.

Green and Schaffer investigated the so-called **tandem method**, which clusters on factor scores, and found that it did not provide any advantages over using the raw data, and could lead to inferior solutions.

Given these considerations, we recommend extreme caution about use of factor scores as basis variables in clustering. They can too easily introduce structures not present in the original data.

4. If you must use factor scores . . .

Many organizations nonetheless insist on using factor scores, instead of simply restricting the basis set to the actual variables loading strongly on each factor (as found in a factor analysis). If you must consider using factor scores, some rules-of-thumb can help you decide whether you can use these scores at all. These involve looking at the percent of variance explained by the significant factors, as follows:

- If these explain over 70% of the total variance, then you MAY want to use the factor scores as the basis variables for clustering. If you can, try clustering the data both ways to see which solution makes the most sense.

- If significant components explain 50% or less of the total variance, then argue hard for using the standardized data.

- If between 50% and 70% explained, it is completely indeterminate—toss a coin.

G. Conjoint and Discrete Choice Utilities as the Basis for Clustering

I. Basics about conjoint analysis

Conjoint analysis is an exercise in which respondents must trade off valuable features vs. each other and decide what they really want, very nearly as in real life. In conjoint, everything must be set up very precisely, as we will see below. As such it is a far more accurate measure of what truly matters than rating scales asking about importances. The basics of conjoint analysis include:

⇒ Breaking a product or service into **attributes** (or features) that can be tested in specific variations (or **levels**),

⇒ Determining how these features are traded off vs. each other when the respondent evaluates a product or service

⇒ Understanding the importances of the features and the influence of changing their levels in a person's decisions

Conjoint traditionally has used special research designs, just like scientific experiments, (most often those called **fractional factorial** or **D-optimal** designs). These allow respondents to rate only a small subset of all combinations of attribute variations or levels. Suppose, for instance, you had four attributes, which could take respectively 4, 4, 3 and 3 levels, as follows for a fictional car study:

Attribute	Engine Size	Price	Country of	Number of Seats
Level 1	81 HP	$18,000	U.S.A.	2
Level 2	102 HP	$20,200	Japan	4
Level 3	117 HP	$22,600	Germany	5
Level 4	154 HP	$24,400		

You could combine these in 144 ways (4 x 4 x 3 x 3). One such configuration might be: 117 horsepower, $10,200 in price, from the USA, with 5 seats. Trying all such configurations could mean 144 alternatives for the respondent to rate—far too many for any normal human being without many recreational substances. Conjoint design methods would allow you to reduce this number sharply—in fact, to 16 product configurations, This would be done by using the specialized **D-optimal** experimental design method. Each of these combinations usually appears on its own card (or screen), and so this could be called an **16-card study.**

Conjoint analysis could then compute the value of all product alternatives, including the many that respondents did not actually rate, from the ratings the respondents did provide.

This type of conjoint analysis called **full profile** conjoint analysis, because respondents rate full **profiles** or descriptions of product alternatives. You may sometimes also see reference to **adaptive, pairwise,** or **hybrid** conjoint, which differ in details of execution and analytical algorithms. However, the basic nature of the output and the uses of the data remain the same.

2. Conjoint analysis output

The output of conjoint analysis programs usually includes:

- **Part-worths** (or **utilities**) for each level of each attribute, for each respondent. Utility is an abstract quantity that reflects the goodness or desirability of each level of each attribute. Utilities can be positive or negative.

- Relative importance weights for the attributes, that is how much each attribute influences the total decision/

- A measure of goodness of fit (sometimes R^2 and sometimes **stress**) that reflects how well the values of alternatives predicted by utilities match the answers provided by the respondent.

  If you get a stress measure with your analysis, less stress is better--as holds elsewhere in your life. Stress values of 0.10 or less are considered acceptable, and values under (about) 0.02 quite good. The maximum value is 1.0. R^2 runs just the opposite, with 1.0 being a perfect score.

3. Critical assumptions

The major assumptions of conjoint analysis include:

⇒ **That the product can be assessed fully as attributes and levels**.

Some products with strong sensory or tactile benefits cannot be evaluated with conjoint. As a colleague has said, "You cannot trade off how good a product tastes." Of course consumers do trade off some sensory benefits for money in the store—but this does not work in a survey. Products like perfume similarly would not be too amenable to testing, unless the variable being varied was price for known brands.

⇒ **That the levels of each independent variable are not too narrow or too broad.**

Respondents, of course, will not be able to distinguish between attribute levels that are too similar to each other. However, separating the attribute levels too much creates similar problems, and can lead to no-contest comparisons.

Determining market segments based on the similarities in individual respondents' utilities often can prove highly useful in understanding a market. The segments often will come out very much like the ones in text books—clearly defined and well separated.

4. Discrete choice modeling vs. conjoint

Discrete choice modeling has become the preferred method for comparing responses to two or more products. Discrete choice typically presents products in a "marketplace environment" side by side, just as they would be in an actual marketplace. Each product can have its own features (or attributes), and these vary, just as in a conjoint exercise. Respondents get to choose, very much as they would in the marketplace, typically with "none of these" as an option. The greater realism of having products appear in a marketplace makes DCM superior to conjoint in matching with how people actually decide.

DCM must go through additional analytical steps to generate individual-level data, using a computer intensive method called **Hierarchical Bayesian** analysis. This can give even the quickest computer quite a workout with a large enough problem.

For all its complexities, DCM finally leads to individual level data that can be handled in a segmentation analysis just as conjoint data is.

5. Brief example based on conjoint analysis

The figures below illustrate the type of linear equations generated by conjoint analysis to represent a respondent's relative weights, or part-worths, for each level of each attribute of a product or service.

In this example, suppose you conducted a conjoint analysis on automobile tires which could have 3 levels of price (P), 3 levels of warranty period (W) and 3 levels of traction (T). Our one equation-based example shows what conjoint utilities might look like for one respondent:

$$U = 3.50\,P_1 + 0.50\,P_2 - 3.00\,P_3 - 2.75\,W_1 - 0.25\,W_2 + 3.00\,W_3 - 4.00\,T_1 + 0.50\,T_2 + 3.50\,T_3$$

The value **U** in this equation represents the respondent's possible total utility or value for any given product configuration. Any given product configuration would have only one **P** term, one **W** term and one **T** term. Comparing the various combinations of **P**, **V** and **T** would lead to an understanding of the respondent's most and least valued product alternatives. This respondent's most favored alternative would consist of P_1, W_3, and T_3.

The coefficients referred to above would then become the basis variables in a clustering routine. This would group together those respondents having similar "part-worth" profiles. That is, this procedure would group together those respondents who viewed the various levels of the attributes in similar ways.

Some writers on conjoint see respondents who rate product/service attribute levels in a similar way as seeking similar **benefits**. There are other possible benefits that a product might have outside attributes that can be directly traded, so this name is not highly descriptive. In fact, other types of benefits can be used as a basis for segmentation. Nonetheless, and somewhat confusingly, some writers refer to this type of conjoint-based segmentation as benefit segmentation.

Using these utilities, you could first find segments, and then compare the overall product preferences of each. You could run simulations within each of the segments, comparing different product configurations, and the likely share (of preference) each would have in competition with the others. A typical market simulator (now most usually an interactive workbook that runs under Microsoft Excel) could include outputs showing the differences in responses for each segment.

Including utilities along with other variables in the basis set means that the utilities must be standardized, as the scales of the other variables will differ. This in theory would cause the sacrifice of some information about the importance of attributes (as larger utilities correspond to more importance). In practice, however, utilities can be mixed with other variables, get standardized, and produce highly useful segmentation schemes.

A note about MaxDiff

MaxDiff is a forced trade-off exercise and so belongs in the same family of methods as conjoint and discrete choice. However, MaxDiff trades individual attributes, by asking a series of questions about which attributes respondents find most and least important. A list of attributes can be shown in sets of 2 to 6. A computer designs the sets of attributes that appear in each comparison. Each attribute must refer to a different idea and together they should not make up an entire product—they could be corporate claims or alternative messages, for instance.

The MaxDiff exercise gets relative importances for the items in the list, and at the ratio level. Therefore, we could say, for instance, that Claim R is four times as important as Claim N. Although the attributes tested by MaxDiff do not compose a product, it generates importances that behave in much the same way as those from the other methods in segmentation.

H. How Many to Sample

Another question about segmentation that is both frequent and difficult to answer concerns how many to sample. In many cases, this means: "How few respondents can I use, and still get worthwhile results?"

Most algorithms, and methods for diagnosing results, in fact require relatively few respondents to produce mathematically significant results. For instance, as an experiment, we conducted a discriminant analysis taking a random sub-sample of 36 respondents from a clustering analysis that led to six segments. The average number in each of our analysis groups therefore was 6. The analysis still found 10 basis variables (out of 15 observed with the larger sample) that significantly discriminated among these very small groups.

Therefore, the more important consideration will be how representative your sample is, not whether it can pass some mathematical criterion. Few professional researchers feel much comfort in making sweeping statements about samples much under 100. This discomfort is well warranted. People of course are highly complex entities, varying in ways we can only glimpse through any questionnaire. Given this great diversity, capturing the range of likely responses requires large numbers. Conducting a study that attempts to classify and group people requires even larger numbers.

The key question becomes what you and your organization can tolerate as a minimum sample for a segment. You cannot expect to find clusters of strictly even size. As one practical guideline, you can expect at least one cluster to be half the size of the other, larger ones. (If all your clusters come out even in size, then you can consider yourself lucky.) You need to weigh this likely variability in cluster size, and how many clusters you expect to find, as a guide to sample size.

For instance, suppose you decide you will not consider any solution that leads to a sample of less than 70 in any cluster. Suppose also that you want to consider up to six segments in your final solution. This means that *at an absolute minimum*, you would set your sample at 70 + (5 x 140) or 770. But here, if you do not have good luck, you could still fail to meet your minimum. A sample of 900 might be better.

Recall that most segmentation studies will get analyzed, at some time, by cross-tabulation. Each segment will form a **banner point.** (That is, each segment will serve as the sample base for a column in the analysis.) If you have a minimum size for a banner point, use this to work backward to a total sample, using a formula like the one above. Try to put in extra respondents to defend against the unpredictable. Stories of unusual results in clustering are legion, so you are best served by being conservative.

As a more concrete guideline, we rarely encounter segmentation done with less than 500 to 600 respondents, even where a simple 3-segment or 4-segment model of the market is the goal. Samples can range up into the thousands, and often will need to become this large if you expect regional variations in segments.

I. Using Discriminant Analysis to Extend Clustering

1. Basics

Discriminant analysis can be highly helpful in interpreting cluster output. As a reminder, this procedure uses the clusters as a **grouping variable**--this is the dependent variable in this form of analysis. It then seeks to find which combinations of basis or other variables most differentiate between the clusters.

Discriminant analysis combines the variables into **dimensions**. Each dimension will contain a collection of variables in an equation like a regression. The strength that each variable has in each dimension, its **coefficient**, can help us see different concerns that are differentiating among the groups. The strongest variables do the most to define the each dimension.

Discriminant analysis can also show how well each cluster has been identified, give detailed information on how much clusters look alike, and even provide each respondent's likelihood of belonging to each cluster group. Discriminant analysis typically gives you a lot more output than a regression. In a large statistics program like SAS or SPSS, you can ask for a great deal of information. We will cover some key items here.

2. How the technique works: examples of discriminant analysis output

The section will use output from the statistical package SPSS to illustrate additional some insights this form of analysis can provide. Other large statistical packages will provide similar information.

a. Matrix of pairwise F ratios drawn from a discriminant analysis

This example shows a solution that is very strong overall. The F-ratios show how much separation there is between each pair of segments. Bigger F values are better—the cutoff for significance at the 95% level is 1.96. All segments are significantly separated. The only two where the test statistic is significant at less than the 0.00 level (99.99% or better) are the Trend seekers (group 4) vs. the Clothes conscious (group 5). You only need the top half of this table (highlighted). Like much that comes from most statistics packages, this has a lot of duplicate information.

Segments	Test values	1 Practicals	2 Apathetics	3 Moderates	4 Trend seekers	5 Clothes conscious	6 Sale seekers
1 Practicals	F		11.08	1022.33	13.00	20.34	19.64
	Sig.		0.00	0.00	0.00	0.00	0.00
2 Apathetics	F	11.08		246.72	13.89	20.16	11.00
	Sig.	0.00		0.00	0.00	0.00	0.00
3 Moderates	F	1022.33	246.72		617.12	972.19	534.47
	Sig.	0.00	0.00		0.00	0.00	0.00
4 Trend seekers	F	13.00	13.89	617.12		2.81	34.91
	Sig.	0.00	0.00	0.00		0.02	0.00
5 Clothes conscious	F	20.34	20.16	972.19	2.81		40.82
	Sig.	0.00	0.00	0.00	0.02		0.00
6 Sale seekers	F	19.64	11.00	534.47	34.91	40.82	
	Sig.	0.00	0.00	0.00	0.00	0.00	

b. Summary table of functions' significances and variance explained

In addition to the significance values, this table shows the **Wilks' Lambda.** Lambda gives a measure of variance explained. Here we see the variance explained as the procedure adds more equations to the mix. The same variables, in this case about 30, form all these functions. The Wilks' Lambda, basically, can be considered as $1-R^2$ (there is a minuscule difference depending on how many functions get formed). When we add get all five functions (in the top row), we are doing quite well, with (1 - 0.010) or 99% of variance explained. However, the fifth function does not add much beyond the fourth. Using just four functions (in row 2) we still explain 94% of the variance. Note that the first function only explains 24.5% of the variance—so the adding extra complexity of more functions does help a great deal with classification

Test of Function(s)	Wilks' Lambda	Chi-square	df	Sig.
1 through 5	.010	15893.5	150	.000
2 through 5	.062	9532.0	116	.000
3 through 5	.227	5081.7	84	.000
4 through 5	.491	2439.9	54	.000
5	.755	965.7	26	.000

c. Discriminant classification table for an entire sample

This table gives highly detailed information about how well segments are separated, based on the best combination of variables that significantly differentiate between the segments. You can run this type of table either with basis variables or with some other set of variables.

This example shows excellent results. Correct classification levels—the percentages whose predicted group matches their actual group, based solely on the equations from the discriminant analysis—are shown with gray highlights. The only area in which group memberships are not predicted at **extremely** good levels is for group 2, where there is some mild confusion with group 3. (13.6% of those predicted to be in group 2 based solely on the discriminant equations actually were in group 3.) Otherwise the worst level of confusion is 7.2% for those in group 2 who would be misclassified as being in group 6. These are particularly good results, showing that the solution, based on using about 30 variables, was very strong.

Classification Results								
Solution with 6 clusters		Predicted Group Membership						
		1	2	3	4	5	6	Total
Actual group membership	1	89.7	1.7	.0	1.1	4.3	3.2	100.0
	2	3.8	74.7	13.6	.0	.7	7.2	100.0
	3	.1	3.2	96.4	.1	.0	.2	100.0
	4	.7	2.2	2.2	91.3	2.5	1.1	100.0
	5	5.0	1.1	.6	.5	86.7	6.0	100.0
	6	1.2	1.9	.0	.1	2.1	94.6	100.0

90.4% correctly classified overall

d. All-group scatter-plot

This plot shows how the groups fall on the first two discriminant dimensions. Since discriminant analysis produced 5 dimensions, you would not necessarily expect to find clusters with clear structures in just the first two dimensions. (What you see in this plot is something like the "shadows" of the clusters from five dimensional space.)

In fact, since this plot does not show three of the five dimensions, the clusters indeed are separated ways we cannot see. That said, although the living black and white below does not show the groups that differently, we can see fairly clear regions. Segment 4 is off on its own even in this plot, and indeed other analyses showed that it differed very strongly from the other groups.

Figure 8: An all-groups scatter-plot

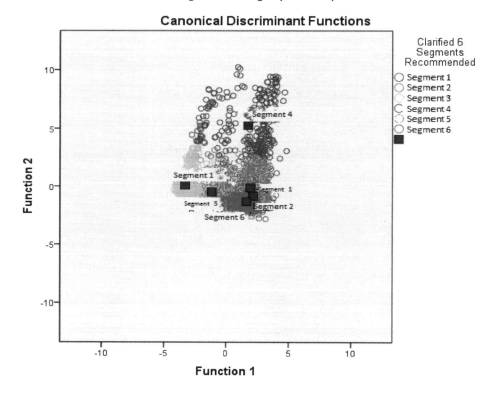

e. Discriminant scores and discriminant correlations

We need to look at both the coefficients, or the weights the variables have in each function, and the correlations each variable has with each function. Each variable's correlation is its similarity in scoring to the score you would get from the total score in the dimension. This may seem confusing, but the extra output is helpful. The coefficients in a discriminant analysis can be distorted, just as they can be in a regression, due to high correlations among variables, or too many (or even too few) variables being in the model. The correlations provide a check on the coefficients.

Therefore we want the variables with strong coefficients in a dimension to have strong correlations with that dimension. We also want the signs of the coefficient and correlation to be pointing in the same direction. When this does not happen, we need to check out the discriminant model. Our first step would be to get rid of the misbehaving variables. However, it may take a number of tries to get everything into good running order. In the example below, with just a few variables, everything worked out very well for us.

Rotated Standardized Canonical Discriminant Function Coefficients [a]

	Function				
	1	2	3	4	5
q14_2 I really keep to the middle of the road	1.005*	.000	.001	.000	.000
q14_9 I will pay more for my favorite brand	.026	.992*	-.124	.226	.033
q14_18 I have sophisticated tastes	.081	.127	1.054*	.054	-.228
q14_10 I dont like to buy expensive things	.023	.135	.040	1.036*	-.141
q14_11 I like to try new brands	.018	.051	-.156	-.118	.910*
q14_12 I only shop if there is a sale	-.011	-.276	.186	.047	.481*

[a]. % of variance by function 1 = 85.8, function 2 = 6.6, function 3 = 3.8, function 4 = 2.2, function 5 = 1.6

We can see (in small type at the bottom) that the strongest differences by far occur in dimension 1, as it has 85.8% of all the variance that is explained by this solution. This does not mean that this dimension has an R-squared of 0.858, just that this dimension explains nearly all the variance that can be explained by this solution. The other dimension are much weaker.

When we see where each group's average score is on each dimension, we then can tell which groups are most strongly differentiated by each. In this simple example, only dimension 5 has more than one variable defining it. That is a combination of liking to try new brands and shopping only if there are sales.

Unfortunately, the table showing the scores needs to go on the next page due to space limitations. It is labeled, rather confusingly, "Functions at Group Centroids." Somewhat more helpfully below, it says, "Unstandardized canonical discriminant functions evaluated at group means." **Centroid** is just a statistical term for the average when a group is plotted in a space. These are just the average scores for each group in each dimension.

Correlations Between Variables and Rotated Functions

	Function				
	1	2	3	4	5
q14_2 I really keep to the middle of the road	.995	-.044	-.080	-.010	-.018
q14_9 I will pay more for my favorite brand	-.003	.952	.179	-.066	.088
q14_18 I have sophisticated tastes	.001	.207	.958	-.096	.052
q14_10 I dont like to buy expensive things	.001	-.182	-.083	.970	.055
q14_11 I like to try new brands	.004	.175	.122	-.018	.864
q14_12 I only shop if there is a sale	-.007	-.353	.187	.278	.478

These dimensions are standardized, so that scores outside the range +/-1 are quite different from the average. We can see that Moderates score very high on Function 1, and the Practicals, Clothes Conscious and Sales Seekers all score very low. (Trend Seekers score quite low, but not as much as the other three.) "I really keep to the middle of the road" defines the first function. That is the only variable with a large coefficient. And this one concern strongly separates one group from the three others. The one which strongly endorses being "middle of the road" is indeed the Moderates.

In fact, the strong opinions of this group led directly to their name—which we created for them. As far as the statistics program is concerned, they are just labeled " Group 1."

Functions at Group Centroids

Segment	Function				
	1	2	3	4	5
1 Practicals	*-1.382*	.198	-.141	-.018	-.119
2 Apathetics	.151	*-.409*	-.198	-.070	*-.391*
3 Moderates	**1.389**	.106	.010	-.056	.053
4 Trend seekers	-.748	**.617**	**.863**	.050	**.296**
5 Clothes conscious	*-1.123*	**.435**	**.384**	-.277	.149
6 Sale seekers	*-1.208*	*-.456*	*-.243*	**.342**	.032

Unstandardized canonical discriminant functions evaluated at group means

Similarly, we can see that on dimension 2, there is still a difference (but not as much of one) between (on one side) the Trend seekers and the Clothes conscious, and (on the other side) the Sale seekers and the Apathetic. This dimension is defined by: "I will pay more for my favorite brand". The Trend seekers and Clothes conscious are willing to do so, while the other two groups are much less interested.

Even though the remaining dimensions explain relatively little variance, we can still trace down other distinctions among the groups in each of them, using the same process of finding high and low scores and looking for the strong variables. This paints a picture of what most strongly distinguishes among the groups. With more variables this story can become highly detailed—and tell a compelling story.

A detailed story, if told well, can capture the attention of an audience

f. The point-vector map and the discriminant territorial map

Since we have coefficients in each function and group averages in each function, it is possible to plot these in a map. In this example, if we plot dimension 1 vs. dimension 2, for instance, Group 1, the Practicals, would fall at -1.382 (x-axis for dimension 1) and 0.198 (the y-axis or dimension 2). The arrow corresponding to "I really keep to the middle of the road" would end at 1.005 on the x-axis and 0.0 on the y-axis. So this concern would point mostly away from the Practicals group.

By repeating this with the other variables and groups, we then can see which concerns tend to point most strongly toward which group. We also see relationships among the groups—note that, for instance, three segments (1, 4 and 5) all fall fairly close to each other, and they are quite far from the Moderates.

This is called a point-vector map because the variables are considered to be **vectors** or something like forces that push the groups to different locations. For instance, the strong score of the Moderates in keeping to "the middle of the road" pushes them to the right on the graph.

This two-dimensional map would explain 92% of the variance of this solution, and nearly all of that (85.8%) would be in the first dimension. In this graph, then, distance along the x-axis shows the strongest differences among the groups. As we can see, careful reading of this chart can provide insights about the groups and what defines and differentiates them.

However, some statistics programs produce a another potentially interesting kind of display, called a territorial map. This map shows the regions, or territories, most clearly associated with each group. A group's territory is that combination of scores where a person is most

Figure 9a: A discriminant point-vector map

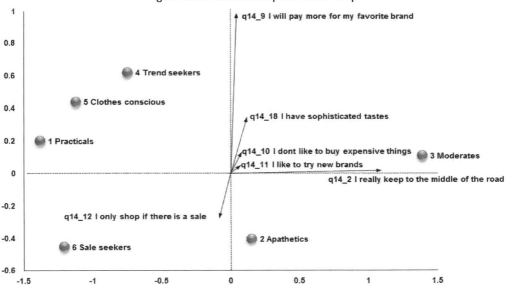

likely to belong to that group.

This means that this map does not show the relative size of the groups. Rather, the height and width of each group in this map represents the range of opinions in that group. (Groups that vary more on a given dimension appear larger on that dimension.) This map does not show how much the groups overlap. Rather, it accentuates the differences between the groups. Putting labels on the dimensions (as follows) can make this a highly informative summary of what differentiates the groups.

Because the last simple example has only one variable per dimension, we will use another example from a study about banking. In this instance, we will have five concerns that differentiate strongly among 4 groups. We will spare you the raw output of the statistics program, which looks like it was produced by an Underwood portable typewriter in about1956. Instead we will show the map traced over this rather quickly in PowerPoint.

When you look at this map, please recall that the sizes of the groups do not reflect the range of opinions not the number in each group. A group with more diversity of opinions will have a larger space, as some in the group agree strongly with the concerns defining a dimension and some disagree strongly. A look at the actual map will help clarify just what this means.

That is, the group at the bottom, "Money Savers" has a wide range of opinions about the concerns represented by the first dimension (valuing commitment, personal service and extra attention). They are strongly defined by the second dimension, where they are pushed toward the bottom by the extent to which they value savings. They similarly do not value speed and efficiency—caring about these concerns would drive them toward the top on the second dimension. In fact, this group's shape and location shows us clearly that all they care about is lower costs.

Similarly, the Premium shoppers are high on valuing commitment, personal service and extra

Figure 9b: A discriminant territorial map

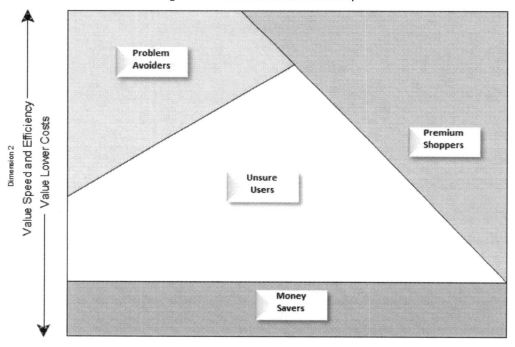

attention—while also being high on valuing speed and efficiency. To get these, they are willing to sacrifice lower costs, valuing which would be opposed to valuing speed and efficiency.

We can tell similar stories about the other groups—and so careful interpretation of a map like this can provide a great many valuable insights about how segments compare and differ.

3. Scoring new respondents into existing clusters

In ongoing classification, respondents often get "scored into" existing cluster groups. That is, they get assigned to groups according to a scheme that was developed in an earlier study, rather than getting assigned based on some new clustering scheme. You would do this if you had a model of now the marketplace segmented and wanted to see how new respondents (perhaps in another area, or at a later time) fit into that model.

You can use discriminant analysis to do this scoring procedure. Using the sample in your original baseline study, you develop a set of **Fisher's discriminant coefficients**. This process will, for each group, generate one coefficient for each variable and a constant term. In the new study, you multiply each respondent's answers by the coefficients, sum these, and add the constant. The group for which the respondent gets the highest total score is the one to which you would assign the respondent.

A simple example follows for one respondent, showing how actual responses get translated into group assignment.

Simple example of group assignment with Fisher's discriminant coefficients

In the table below, the response is repeated before each coefficient for ease in following the calculations. Whatever the numerical value of the response, it gets multiplied by a complete set of coefficients for each group. If you had five such groups in your original solution, you would have five such sets of coefficients.

The respondent gets assigned to the one group in which her total score is the highest. This respondent would get assigned to Group 1. Note that the total for Group 3 is not much lower. In this case, the respondent is just slightly more likely to belong to Group 1 than Group 3.

Scoring by this means can be included in an interactive model that runs under Microsoft Excel. In such a model, the Fisher's discriminant functions run behind the scenes. Users get to either type in answers or use controls, and their answers lead to segment assignments. These **typing tools** provide a valuable aid for recruiting people for post-study in-depth interviews or ethnographic research, which can add depth and detail to the portraits of members in each segment The figure below shows a portion of a simple Excel-based scoring or typing tool.

Please recall that for a discriminant-based scoring model to work well, you must have

Variable	(Response)	Coefficient for Group 1	(Response)	Coefficient for Group 2	(Response)	Coefficient for Group 3
Question 1	-5	0.1	-5	0.7	-5	0.3
Question 2	-2	1	-2	0.5	-2	0.1
Question 3	-10	-0.05	-10	0	-10	0.2
Question 4	-6	0.3	-6	-1	-6	0.4
Constant		6		7		2
Sum		8.8		5.5		8.1

questionnaire questions that are easily extracted from the whole questionnaire—including from the context of questions around them. For this reason, methods such as conjoint or discrete choice do not produce output that can be used in this type of scoring model.

Figure 10: A part of an interactive scoring model or typing tool

You MUST click on or use EACH control each time you run the sheet						Enter ID
How much do you agree with each of these statements?	Disagree Strongly	Disagree Somewhat	Neither	Agree Somewhat	Agree Strongly	12
I always want to try the latest therapy	○	⦿	○	○	○	2
I am very satisfied with the healthcare I receive	○	○	⦿	○	○	3
If I take the right actions, I can stay healthy	○	○	○	⦿	○	4
Following doctor orders to the letter is best	○	○	○	○	○	4
I like to take as few prescription medications as possible	○	○	⦿	○	○	3
	Not at all likely	Somewhat likely	Likely	Very likely	Extremely likely	
How likely would you be the switch to a new drug if it was purer in composition and manufacture?	○	○	○	⦿	○	4
	Not at all	Not very	Some-what	Very	Extremely	
How influential is the nurse or the nurse practitioner in your therapy decision?	○	○	⦿	○	○	3
	Clicking on arrow moves one unit; clicking on band inside arrow moves 10 units					
What is your current age in years? (Please slide the control to get the correct age)	◄				►	70
How satisfied are you with your current therapy? (Please use a 0 to100 scale, where 0 means completely unsatisfied and 100 means completely satisfied)	◄				►	100

FORECASTED SEGMENT	Open
Strength of membership	Strong
Probability "Open" segment	69%
Probability "Disaffected" segment	31%
Probability "Engaged" segment	0%

4. Discriminant analysis versus multinomial logit

Multinomial logit can perform many of the same analyses as discriminant analysis. However, in theory, it has some advantages. Discriminant analysis has among its basic assumptions that the independent (basis) variables have normal distributions and equal variances. Logit does not make these assumptions about the data. However, in practice, discriminant analysis is extremely **robust.** That is, it still works well even when the data do not meet its basic assumptions. At worst, it may have some trouble with the correct classification of the "marginal" respondents who do not clearly fit into any group.

One advantage multinomial logit has over discriminant analysis is that it provides coefficients for each variable within each group or cluster. These can be translated into **odds**—and that may have appeal to some audiences. Disadvantages of multinomial logit mostly relate to its relative unfamiliarity. The findings typically seem confusing and so require additional explanation. Lastly, its output does not lend itself as readily to mapping or to creating interactive scoring models as does the output from discriminant analysis.

J. Selecting the Number of Segments

1. Fundamental issues

Some of these issues are mathematical, others that could be called managerial. The mathematical issues would include:

- Power of the clusters to "explain" the data,
- Stability of the segments,
- Segment distinctiveness,
- Segment homogeneity.

Unfortunately, no easy answers have arisen for these problems, as the following sections will describe. Other issues largely concern the **managerial cost** of segmentation. Managerial cost simply means the expense of actually using the plan. Organizations may launch into complex schemes with more than a primary and secondary target audience, for instance, only to find the weight of making many simultaneous efforts overwhelming.

2. The mathematical problems, and one preliminary approach

Although many have tried to determine statistically the optimum number of clusters in a cluster analysis, no procedure has gained general acceptance and none seems applicable to every clustering problem you might encounter. We now have some procedures, such as certain variants of latent class clustering, X-means clustering and SPSS TwoStep clustering, that will make recommendations based on their own criteria.

These recommendations often are right on the money However, you are always best served by examining some alternative solutions to make sure. Selecting the right number of clusters ultimately still depends on the judgment of the analyst.

One method that has gained some support, and indeed that has been incorporated into a product producing clusters by latent classes, is to examine the percent of **variance explained** (pattern in the data explained) by each cluster solution from 2 groups to the maximum. You can try this within a given form of clustering if your algorithm gives some measure of the variance explained by each solution. To do this, you need to graph the percent of variance explained by each solution. A so-called **knee** in this graph **may** show where the percent of variance explained starts to decrease, relative to the formation of new clusters.

However, **no single mathematical test**, or combination of tests, will supplant the need to examine solutions carefully—as we showed how to do in earlier sections.

Figure 11: Percent of variance explained in adding clusters

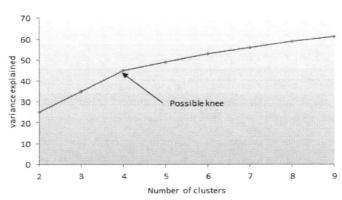

3. Discriminant analysis approaches to selecting the number of clusters

Simply running a discriminant analysis for each cluster solution will often help you select one that seems best. We have seen how you can do this by inspecting the various statistics produced by the analysis of each solution, including:

- Wilks' Lambda,
- pair-wise F-ratios,
- the percent of each group classified correctly, and
- overall correct classification.

The all-group scatter plot may help you determine if the solution has a clear structure. (Keep in mind the cautions about this already mentioned—if the solution has more than two dimensions, looking at only two can make the picture look cloudy.) Looking at which variables actually discriminate most between the groups (looking at the rotated coefficients of each variable, for instance) can help you decide which solution makes the most sense.

4. Using hold-out samples

A **hold-out sample** usually means a portion of your total sample (usually 25% -40%) that you set aside while you classify the rest of the respondents. Another newer method of holding out—one that seems quite stringent—is called **cross folding.** We will discuss each in turn.

The most commonly-used approach involves classifying the hold-out sample with the classification scheme developed on the rest of the sample. You can do this simply, if not automatically, with any of the larger statistical packages (SPSS, SAS, Systat, etc.), as follows. The method involves "setting aside" 25% to 40% of all respondents as a holdout sample, running the analysis excluding this group, and developing a classification scheme that is then applied to that group.

- In SPSS, the hardest part may be remembering to specify that you want a "temporary" sample before you draw it. While SPSS has a wonderful system for drawing commands from menus, this step is done most efficiently using syntax. Simply first type the command "Temporary." (Use no quotes but include the period.)

- Then type the command "Sample" and some decimal amount from 0 to 1. Taking a sample of 75% would use "Sample 0.75." (Again use no quotes but use the closing period.) This temporary sample is what you use to develop your model.

- After you have run the model, classify the holdout sample, using the scheme developed on the rest of the sample. Examine the results referring to both the percent of each group classified correctly, and any groups that have a relatively high misclassification rate. Consider groups with high misclassifications as candidates for consolidation with other clusters.

- If the holdout sample is not well classified (that is, less than, say, 60% correct), then clearly defined clusters may not exist in the data. You may need to try clustering with a new set of basis variables.

The more stringent form of holding out that we mentioned, **cross-folding**, works by splitting the sample into a number of randomly drawn fractions. Ten-fold cross-folding would divide the sample in ten, develop the model on 9/10 of the sample, and then test it on the remaining 1/10. It would then do this 9 more times, and would average the ten tests for a correct classification level. Your sample must be large to use 10-fold cross-folding. With a smaller sample you might just fold 5 times or 4 times for instance.

5. Investigating the stability of segments

Investigating the **stability** or **stabilization** of segments can also help determine when to stop splitting the sample into more clusters. You can do this type of investigation easily if your clustering program produces a **crossover matrix**. This matrix simply shows how respondents migrate from cluster to cluster in successive solutions, as you add more groups.

- The aim of this is to infer when a given clustering algorithm has finished finding true structures in the data set, and then begins forming additional clusters simply because you have instructed it to continue.

As you add groups, you usually will see larger groups breaking apart fairly cleanly. What "fairly cleanly" means is quite subjective. However, the disintegration that can happen as you add one group too many can be quite dramatic. You might go from, for instance, six to seven clusters, and for the first time see a group formed of small pieces of several clusters that have held fairly steady through all the earlier tries.

Otherwise, you can look at the means of each group on the basis variables. Check to see if these means hold steady for established clusters as you increase the number of groups. Once these means appear to shift strongly for many variables, your solution has probably become unstable.

There are no hard and fast statistical tests, simply judgment.

6. Investigating segment homogeneity versus number of segments

As clustering procedures form more segments, the segments usually become more homogeneous. However, as you add more segments, the more non-target segments you are likely to encounter. And as you find more non-target segments, targets may diminish in size. (As a reminder, segmentation does not take place so that we can market to all groups but in different ways—but rather so we can focus on the most valuable groups.)

You therefore must balance the need for finding highly homogeneous groups against the real-world need to restrict the number of clusters. Following (in Figure 11) is the cluster homogeneity index for each cluster found in solutions ranging from 2 to 9 groups. You can see the number of groups in the left-most column. The index simply compares the variance within each cluster to the overall variance (of the entire sample). You therefore want to find low homogeneity indexes with this procedure.

In the chart below, one cluster in each solution has higher variance than the entire sample. How much of a problem this poses depends on the size of the cluster in question. You might even exclude the individuals in this "cluster" from your analysis, if there are just a few of them, since they form a relatively non-cohesive group.

The problematic cluster in each solution appears highlighted. This is cluster 1 for between 2 and 6 clusters, then cluster 7 for more clusters. Very possibly this is the same group, just moved to a different cluster number for unknown and likely random reasons.

7. Comparing many solutions

Almost any statistics program allows you to run more than one type of clustering. Comparing solutions from several methods can help you find the most effective clustering scheme while gaining insights into the data. This can be cumbersome to do, but it is critical for finding the best solution. Unfortunately, some methods that routinely are strong methods are largely hidden in some statistics packages. For instance, the process of **seeding K-Means clustering** on SPSS is

Homogeneity Index for each Cluster

Break	1	2	3	4	5	6	7	8	9
2	1.054	0.632							
3	1.16	0.486	0.803						
4	1.13	0.461	0.743	0.775					
5	1.135	0.441	0.724	0.72	0.696				
6	1.124	0.482	0.73	0.728	0.727	0.388			
7	0.933	0.494	0.686	0.704	0.74	0.39	1.176		
8	0.912	0.506	0.7	0.71	0.757	0.334	1.205	0.49	
9	0.919	0.468	0.687	0.71	0.765	0.334	1.205	0.498	0.619

very roundabout. **Seeding** means starting with a small sample, running one of the hierarchical methods, and then saving the group averages. These averages form the starting points for K-Means clusters. These calculated starting points often work better than the default random start points that the programs use.

Following is some output from a custom application that does a great deal of the hard work. This output unfortunately is not available from the major statistical packages. Still, reading this will give some ideas about what you can try. Figure 12a lists the runs done aiming for 4 clusters. There are other runs for 3 clusters and 5 to 8 clusters. At the top, we see how many variables are involved and what the total sample was. We see that standardization was used. Also there was no **centering** within respondents—which would take each respondent's answers and rescale them so that they have a mean of zero and a standard deviation of one. We did not do anything extra to remove scaling and did not weight the data. The distance metric is **squared**, meaning that we take into account all the distances among respondents and transform those so that they are all compared on a positive scale.

There are 13 type of clustering here. Each type of clustering is called a **replication.** We have simple K-Means, both distance based and density based; then simple K-means with seeding by three kinds of hierarchical methods (single linkage or SLINK, complete linkage or CLINK and Wards.) Next we have the same five variants for another type of K-

Figure 12a; Initial output from a program comparing many solutions

Clusters	Variables	Observations	Standardized	Centered	emoved Scalir	Weighted	Measure
4	30	399	N-1 Std Dev	NO	NO	NO	Squared-Euclidean

List of Replications Performed

Number	Method	Specifics	Solution Name
1	IK Means-simple (Forgy)	Distance based	Solution 2 [1,4]
2	IK Means-simple (Forgy)	Density based	Solution 7 [2,4]
3	IK Means-simple (Forgy)	Hierarchical SLINK	Solution 12 [3,4]
4	IK Means-simple (Forgy)	Hierarchical CLINK	Solution 17 [4,4]
5	IK Means-simple (Forgy)	Hierarchical WARDs	Solution 22 [5,4]
6	IK Means-reflected (Jancey)	Distance based	Solution 27 [6,4]
7	IK Means-reflected (Jancey)	Density based	Solution 32 [7,4]
8	IK Means-reflected (Jancey)	Hierarchical SLINK	Solution 37 [8,4]
9	IK Means-reflected (Jancey)	Hierarchical CLINK	Solution 42 [9,4]
10	IK Means-reflected (Jancey)	Hierarchical WARDs	Solution 47 [10,4]
11	Hierarchical agglomerative	Nearest Neighbor SLINK	Solution 52 [11,4]
12	Hierarchical agglomerative	Farthest Neighbor CLINK	Solution 57 [12,4]
13	Hierarchical agglomerative	Minimal Variance (Ward)	Solution 62 [13,4]

Means called **reflected** or Jancey. Finally, we have three types of hierarchical clustering—the same ones used to do the **seeding** for the K-Means approach.

We see in the next table (or perhaps would see if the type were larger) how each solution compares to all the others in assigning respondents to clusters. In very small figures, it shows that on average solution 1 put respondents into the same clusters as all the other methods some 65.66% of the time. This is not a particularly good score, but it is brought down by this solution having little in common with the hierarchical methods (replicates 11 to 13 are the hierarchical methods).

The best of the 13 alternatives in this area are numbers 9 and 10 at 80.99% correct and 80.89% correct on average overall. These alternatives also align worst when compared with the hierarchical methods. As a reminder, regardless of method, we had exactly the same basis variables and the same basic rules for analysis. This underlines how important the choice of algorithm can be in the results that you finally obtain.

As we will see on the next pages, this is just the beginning—the solutions will get compared on a wide range of criteria. Following in Figure 12c we have another grid with, in this format, very small numbers. This is a much more thorough comparison of the clusters using a number of criteria.

Figure 12b: Initial recommendations and comparison of solutions

Best replication for the 4 cluster solutions was replication 1.
(Look for cells with this background color.)

Best over all solution was the 4 cluster solution generated by replication 1.
(Look for cells with this background color.)

Pairwise Reproducibility of Replicates

Replication	1	2	3	4	5	6	7	8	9	10	11	12	13
1		75.44	70.43	71.43	65.41	73.18	69.42	68.17	75.19	75.69	36.59	36.34	70.68
2	75.44		80.20	87.22	88.97	95.49	90.23	88.72	97.74	98.50	35.09	53.88	69.17
3	70.43	80.20		90.98	88.22	80.70	88.72	87.22	81.20	80.95	38.85	62.66	54.64
4	71.43	87.22	90.98		81.95	86.97	86.72	81.70	88.97	88.22	38.60	63.41	61.65
5	65.41	88.97	88.22	81.95		91.23	93.73	97.99	90.73	90.48	36.84	55.64	57.89
6	73.18	95.49	80.70	86.97	91.23		90.98	91.23	97.49	96.74	34.34	54.64	66.92
7	69.42	90.23	88.72	86.72	93.73	90.98		92.73	91.98	91.23	36.09	58.15	54.64
8	68.17	88.72	87.22	81.70	97.99	91.23	92.73		90.48	90.23	35.59	55.64	56.89
9	75.19	97.74	81.20	88.97	90.73	97.49	91.98	90.48		99.25	35.59	54.89	68.42
10	75.69	98.50	80.95	88.22	90.48	96.74	91.23	90.23	99.25		36.09	54.14	69.17
11	36.59	35.09	38.85	38.60	36.84	34.34	36.09	35.59	35.59	36.09		51.88	50.13
12	36.34	53.88	62.66	63.41	55.64	54.64	58.15	55.64	54.89	54.14	51.88		42.61
13	70.68	69.17	54.64	61.65	57.89	66.92	54.64	56.89	68.42	69.17	50.13	42.61	
Average	65.66	80.05	75.40	77.32	78.26	79.99	78.72	78.05	80.99	80.89	38.81	53.65	60.23

The first column, replication, refers to the type of clustering solution by number. We can go back to the first table and see that 1 is Simple K-Means, 9 is Reflected K-Means seeded with Complete Linkage Hierarchical Clustering, 10 is Reflected K-Means seeded with Ward's method, and 11 is Complete Linkage Hierarchical Clustering done by itself.

Reproducibility shows the best scoring model from the table we saw in Figure 12b. The next four columns show significance measures. These most often agree with each other, although you will notice that pooled significance here turns up a different winner than the other related measures.

Separation and **Density** in this program work differently than the homogeneity scores we saw earlier. **Balance** is a measure of how evenly sized the clusters are. For all three measures, a higher score is a better one.

The solution selected as best was arrived at by weights the analyst decided on for each of the criteria. The most weight was put on pooled F-ratio and mean F-ratio—and on that basis, number 1 was declared optimal. If the weights had been different 9, 10 or 11 could have won. The areas in which each of these three did best rarely get the most weight, though. You might put more weight on balance if you have a small sample and are hoping to find even-sized clusters. However, the pooled F-ratio is a very good summary of the overall goodness of the solution.

Still, we need to look at more than just these summary statistics. Most important of all is whether the solution is useful and whether it makes sense. These criteria are based squarely on judgment.

To help us determine whether the chosen solution makes sense, we need at least some summary information on the clusters. Following is some provided by the same program, but you can do these summaries with relatively little effort yourself.

Figure 12c: Detailed Comparative Output

Best Replication by Criteria Categories

Criteria	Repli-cation	Repro-ducibility	Pooled F Ratio	Pooled Sig	Mean F Ratio	Mean Sig	Bal-anced	Separa-tion	Density
Reproducibility	9	80.99	39.67	0.00	41.55	0.17	62.21	89.54	87.52
Pooled F Ratio	1	65.66	48.84	0.00	55.92	0.05	69.51	89.87	87.10
Pooled Sig	10	80.89	39.66	0.00	41.53	0.17	61.76	89.55	87.52
Mean F Ratio	1	65.66	48.84	0.00	55.92	0.05	69.51	89.87	87.10
Mean Sig	1	65.66	48.84	0.00	55.92	0.05	69.51	89.87	87.10
Balanced	1	65.66	48.84	0.00	55.92	0.05	69.51	89.87	87.10
Separation	11	38.81	5.37	0.00	21.02	0.34	0.00	98.32	96.33
Density	11	38.81	5.37	0.00	21.02	0.34	0.00	98.32	96.33
Combined	1	65.66	48.84	0.00	55.92	0.05	69.51	89.87	87.10
Best 4 cluster	1	65.66	48.84	0.00	55.92	0.05	69.51	89.87	87.10

Again in type that is quite small in this format, following is a table showing the sizes of the clusters and the significance of the variables that differentiate among them. We find one small cluster—group 2, which has 70 individuals. It is on the borderline of being too small a sample to read accurately, and if that group emerges as the best audience for this service, it likely would be too small to serve as an effective target. Typically, for many goods and services, we do find some variant of the "20/80" rule works—namely that 20% of the total population uses about 80% of the product/service. (Of course, this could be 30% using 70% or something similar.) However, a group that is not much over 10% would have to use a tremendous amount of product to become a worthwhile target.

The sizes of the groups therefore give the first level of information about whether the solution will prove to be useful.

We also can see from this table that nearly all the variables we chose for this run are significant. There are only four that do not significantly differentiate the groups (they have no highlighting). It is possible that removing these and trying again will improve the clarity of the solution somewhat. Useless variables at best muddy the findings and at worst may impede us from finding a strong solution.

Following in Figure 12e comes some critical output for seeing whether the solution will work well. These are two of four tables that were generated, one for each group. In each, the scores for the group are arranged from high to low. Using charts like these we can quickly see the "hot buttons" for each group—and what they find unappealing or less useful relative to the other clusters. If these patterns of responses form strongly coherent and useful portrayals, this could be the solution to use.

Figure 12d. Output showing how segments compare overall

		Segmentation Report							
		Replication 1 for 4 Cluster Solution							
Clusters	Iterations	Replication	Method	Specifics	Solution Name				
4	9	1	K Means-simp	Distance base	Solution 2 [1,4]				

Cluster Means and F Ratios

			Cluster Number	1	2	3	4	F Ratio
			Cluster Name	Cl1	Cl2	Cl3	Cl4	
			Cluster Size	174	70	110	145	48.84
1	NUM_S19	NUM_S19 NUM_S19		-0.09	0.24	-0.02	-0.06	1.71
2	Q11	Q11 Thinking only about the appeal of the feature itself, and not about the potential c		0.76	-0.92	-0.26	0.25	56.17
3	Q16	Q16 Overall, how would you rate for being new and different compared to other se		0.72	-0.92	-0.37	0.36	64.05
4	Q21	Q21 Thinking only about the appeal of the feature itself, and not about the potential c		0.86	-0.91	-0.17	0.13	56.54
5	Q26	Q26 Overall, how would you rate for being new and different compared to other se		0.83	-1.00	-0.26	0.26	70.31
6	Q31	Q31 Thinking only about the appeal of the feature itself, and not about the potential c		0.68	-1.11	-0.29	0.41	83.66
7	Q36	Q36 Overall, how would you rate for being new and different compared to other se		0.65	-1.25	-0.25	0.46	106.78
8	Q41	Q41 Thinking only about the appeal of the feature itself, and not about the potential c		0.70	-0.78	-0.02	0.03	32.90
9	Q42	Q42 % more I would have paid for a server with Disk and Network I/O Bottleneck Re		-0.22	0.92	-0.14	-0.23	29.61
10	Q44	Q44 Below is a list of statements that may or may not explain why is appealing for		-0.03	0.13	-0.13	0.05	1.19
11	Q45_2_1	Q45_2_1 Does not apply to me I would not buy this server typeservers where great		0.66	-0.23	-0.17	-0.10	14.94
12	Q45_2_2	Q45_2_2 Does not apply to me I would not buy this server typeservers where great		0.61	-0.21	-0.11	-0.12	12.50
13	Q45_2_3	Q45_2_3 Does not apply to me I would not buy this server typeservers that run mult		0.63	-0.22	-0.11	-0.13	13.37
14	Q45_2_4	Q45_2_4 Does not apply to me I would not buy this server typeservers that follow a		0.49	-0.33	0.00	-0.09	9.37
15	Q46	Q46 Overall, how would you rate for being new and different compared to other se		0.70	-0.97	-0.21	0.27	54.68
16	Q51	Q51 Thinking only about the appeal of the feature itself, and not about the potential c		0.93	-1.07	-0.16	0.16	80.73
17	Q56	Q56 Overall, how would you rate for being new and different compared to other se		0.87	-1.08	-0.24	0.26	83.38
18	Q61	Q61 Thinking only about the appeal of the feature itself, and not about the potential c		0.88	-1.11	-0.15	0.20	81.60
19	Q66	Q66 Overall, how would you rate for being new and different compared to other se		0.80	-1.15	-0.22	0.32	87.99
20	Q71	Q71 Thinking only about the appeal of the feature itself, and not about the potential c		0.31	-1.05	-0.43	0.68	99.56
21	Q86	Q86 Overall, how would you rate for being new and different compared to other se		0.69	-1.01	-0.23	0.31	60.83
22	WEIGHT	Weighting based on org size Small, Medium, Large & Very large		-0.12	0.22	-0.10	0.03	1.89
23	PREDICT	Predictive server error detection and root cause determination		-0.63	0.12	-0.67	0.77	92.89
24	POWER	Power optimized server		-0.60	0.16	-0.64	0.72	78.00
25	VERIFIED	Verified boot and configuration		-0.45	0.31	-0.67	0.59	58.08
26	DISKBOT	Disk and network I/O bottleneck reduction		-0.42	0.04	-0.63	0.68	59.80
27	AUTOP	Automated power and thermal management		-0.71	0.22	-0.68	0.77	107.44
28	RESUSE	Resource usage metering		-0.52	0.27	-0.82	0.76	111.39
29	SECURE	Secure two-way authentication		0.04	0.00	-0.07	0.03	0.25
30	AUTOSV	Automatic server provisioning		-0.30	0.10	-0.74	0.67	66.06

Figure 12e: Summary output about individual clusters

Means as Deviations from Grand Means and F Ratios

Variables Sorted by Cluster's Means as Deviations from Grand Means

Cl1 (Cluster 1 of 4) for Solution 2 [1,4] (Replication 1) containing 174 individuals.

			Grand Means	Mean
16	Q51	Q51: ::Thinking only about the appeal of the feature itself, and not about the potentia	0.00	0.93
18	Q61	Q61: ::Thinking only about the appeal of the feature itself, and not about the potentia	0.00	0.88
17	Q56	Q56: ::Overall, how would you rate for being new and different compared to other	0.00	0.87
4	Q21	Q21: ::Thinking only about the appeal of the feature itself, and not about the potentia	0.00	0.86
5	Q26	Q26: ::Overall, how would you rate for being new and different compared to other	0.00	0.83
19	Q66	Q66: ::Overall, how would you rate for being new and different compared to other	0.00	0.80
2	Q11	Q11: ::Thinking only about the appeal of the feature itself, and not about the potentia	0.00	0.76
3	Q16	Q16: ::Overall, how would you rate for being new and different compared to other	0.00	0.72
8	Q41	Q41: ::Thinking only about the appeal of the feature itself, and not about the potentia	0.00	0.70
15	Q46	Q46: ::Overall, how would you rate for being new and different compared to other	0.00	0.70
21	Q86	Q86: ::Overall, how would you rate for being new and different compared to other	0.00	0.69
6	Q31	Q31: ::Thinking only about the appeal of the feature itself, and not about the potentia	0.00	0.68
11	Q45 2 1	Q45 2 1: Does not apply to me: I would not buy this server type::servers where gr	0.00	0.66
7	Q36	Q36: ::Overall, how would you rate for being new and different compared to other	0.00	0.65
13	Q45 2 3	Q45 2 3: Does not apply to me: I would not buy this server type::servers that run m	0.00	0.63
12	Q45 2 2	Q45 2 2: Does not apply to me: I would not buy this server type::servers where gr	0.00	0.61
14	Q45 2 4	Q45 2 4: Does not apply to me: I would not buy this server type::servers that follow	0.00	0.49
20	Q71	Q71: ::Thinking only about the appeal of the feature itself, and not about the potentia	0.00	0.31
29	SECURE	Secure two-way authentication	0.00	0.04
10	Q44	Q44: ::Below is a list of statements that may or may not explain why is appealing fo	0.00	-0.03
1	NUM S19	NUM S19: ::NUM S19	0.00	-0.09
22	WEIGHT	Weighting based on org size: Small, Medium, Large & Very large	0.00	-0.12
9	Q42	Q42: % more I would have paid for a server with Disk and Network I/O Bottleneck R	0.00	-0.22
30	AUTOSV	Automatic server provisioning	0.00	-0.30
26	DISKBOT	Disk and network I/O bottleneck reduction	0.00	-0.42
25	VERIFIED	Verified boot and configuration	0.00	-0.45
28	RESUSE	Resource usage metering	0.00	-0.52
24	POWER	Power optimized server	0.00	-0.60
23	PREDICT	Predictive server error detection and root cause determination	0.00	-0.63
27	AUTOP	Automated power and thermal management	0.00	-0.71

Cl2 (Cluster 2 of 4) for Solution 2 [1,4] (Replication 1) containing 70 individuals.

			Grand Means	Mean
9	Q42	Q42: % more I would have paid for a server with Disk and Network I/O Bottleneck R	0.00	0.92
25	VERIFIED	Verified boot and configuration	0.00	0.31
28	RESUSE	Resource usage metering	0.00	0.27
1	NUM S19	NUM S19: ::NUM S19	0.00	0.24
27	AUTOP	Automated power and thermal management	0.00	0.22
22	WEIGHT	Weighting based on org size: Small, Medium, Large & Very large	0.00	0.22
24	POWER	Power optimized server	0.00	0.16
10	Q44	Q44: ::Below is a list of statements that may or may not explain why is appealing fo	0.00	0.13
23	PREDICT	Predictive server error detection and root cause determination	0.00	0.12
30	AUTOSV	Automatic server provisioning	0.00	0.10
26	DISKBOT	Disk and network I/O bottleneck reduction	0.00	0.04
29	SECURE	Secure two-way authentication	0.00	0.00
12	Q45 2 2	Q45 2 2: Does not apply to me: I would not buy this server type::servers where gr	0.00	-0.21
13	Q45 2 3	Q45 2 3: Does not apply to me: I would not buy this server type::servers that run m	0.00	-0.22
11	Q45 2 1	Q45 2 1: Does not apply to me: I would not buy this server type::servers where gr	0.00	-0.23
14	Q45 2 4	Q45 2 4: Does not apply to me: I would not buy this server type::servers that follow	0.00	-0.33
8	Q41	Q41: ::Thinking only about the appeal of the feature itself, and not about the potentia	0.00	-0.78
4	Q21	Q21: ::Thinking only about the appeal of the feature itself, and not about the potentia	0.00	-0.91
3	Q16	Q16: ::Overall, how would you rate for being new and different compared to other	0.00	-0.92
2	Q11	Q11: ::Thinking only about the appeal of the feature itself, and not about the potentia	0.00	-0.92
15	Q46	Q46: ::Overall, how would you rate for being new and different compared to other	0.00	-0.97
5	Q26	Q26: ::Overall, how would you rate for being new and different compared to other	0.00	-1.00
21	Q86	Q86: ::Overall, how would you rate for being new and different compared to other	0.00	-1.01
20	Q71	Q71: ::Thinking only about the appeal of the feature itself, and not about the potentia	0.00	-1.05
16	Q51	Q51: ::Thinking only about the appeal of the feature itself, and not about the potentia	0.00	-1.07
17	Q56	Q56: ::Overall, how would you rate for being new and different compared to other	0.00	-1.08
18	Q61	Q61: ::Thinking only about the appeal of the feature itself, and not about the potentia	0.00	-1.11
6	Q31	Q31: ::Thinking only about the appeal of the feature itself, and not about the potentia	0.00	-1.11
19	Q66	Q66: ::Overall, how would you rate for being new and different compared to other	0.00	-1.15
7	Q36	Q36: ::Overall, how would you rate for being new and different compared to other	0.00	-1.25

80

K. Profiling and Locating the Segments

1. Overview

Profiling, or describing, segments typically extends beyond the basis variables used in the clustering routine. Profiling can be descriptive, creating a portrait of a group that helps broaden understanding or bring the group to life. Profiling also leads to an all-important third element of segmentation—making groups selectively reachable—as outlined in Section I (part D). This part of profiling involves action-oriented variables that appear in the survey but do not get used as basis variables.

Profiling procedures could include any of the following:

- Cross-tabulation
- Classification trees
- Discriminant analysis
- Logit (and probit) analysis

Most usually profiling involves cross-tabulation. This likely is the most prevalent form of output that follows any segmentation study—and perhaps nearly every market research study except for trade-off exercises such as conjoint and discrete choice, where the key output is market simulations.

The type of profiling which comprises the creation of a portrait or narrative that describes the segments can reach across all variables. Such descriptions can involve numbers or words only—we will show examples of each.

Action-oriented profiling requires variables that the organization can use to reach people selectively. The exact nature of these would depend on what the organization can find and use in connection with its customers and its prospects. Examples of action-oriented profiling variables would include such descriptors as:

$\Rightarrow$ Media Usage
$\Rightarrow$ Brand Usage
$\Rightarrow$ Web usage
$\Rightarrow$ Demographics
$\Rightarrow$ Various "life style" variables.

All of these types of profiling variables can be added or appended to a database of customers and prospects by various organizations, such as Acxiom or InfoAmerica. There is a wealth of information on nearly every household in the United States. Although some of the information is spotty, the overall quantity is staggering.

The most powerful means of action-oriented profiling involves the use of classification tree methods (CHAID, CRT and so on). These methods provide so many strong benefits that we will spend Part M (following) explaining how they can be used.

Logit and probit rarely get used in profiling research reports. Therefore, the sections following will discuss strengths and weaknesses of cross-tabulation and discriminant analysis in profiling segments—and then we will get to the main discussion of classification trees.

2. Profiling with cross-tabulation procedures

How this gets done

This likely is familiar to anybody who has ever worked on a research report. In segmentation, specifically, the cluster groups become the **banner points** (column-defining variables) in a standard cross-tabulation. There may be further cross-tabulations, such as defining columns by age groups within clusters, geographies within clusters, clusters within age groups, clusters within geographies, age groups within clusters within geographies, and more combinations involving age, income, education, life stage, life styles, and so on.

Usually, all variables in the study become the row variables or **stubs.** This can lead to a very large number of tables to read and consider. This seems to be done almost entirely electronically now. There was a time when a stack of enormous binders holding cross-tabulations (in tiny type) was almost a badge of honor. Those days seem largely gone.

Pros and cons

The **advantages** are well known and make cross-tabs ubiquitous. They are easy and economical to execute. They provide a basic level of description that is easy to understand. Finally, nearly everybody expects a set of these as part of a study.

First among **disadvantages**, as we suggested at the top of the page, you typically get very large amounts of output. Cross-tabs are notoriously time-consuming to wade through and analyze. In many ways, the ease of cross-tabs works against them—it is simple to ask for another set of banner points, and another. The wealth of comparisons being drawn, typically across every response given, can decline into hypothesis-free examination. In data mining circles, this is called **data dredging.** It can become a lot of work with little return.

The major cross-tabulation packages remain surprisingly weak at statistical tests for significant differences. Some tests offered do particularly poorly when comparing several columns of data—where special tests are needed—the more familiar t-test (or z-test) becomes inaccurate as it is designed for comparing only two columns, . One major tabulation package offers nothing more than a test it calls "Newman-Keuls," apparently a weakened version of the **SNK** or **Student-Newman-Keuls**, one of the earliest and most fallible tests for comparing more than two groups at one time.

Beyond this, widespread use of the wrong tests persists. Many analysts continue to apply ordinary t-tests to as many as a dozen (or more) comparisons within a single set of cross-tabbed columns. (Again, t-tests are intended only for comparing two columns at a time) By the way, six columns in a set can be compared 12 different ways two at a time. There's a formula that tells us this, although more enthusiastic readers could check manually. Making a lot of comparisons in this way can result in falsely finding spurious differences.

Finally, cross-tabs consider just two variables at a time—column header vs. row variable. They will not identify themes in the data or paint as concise and precise a picture of the segments as multivariate methods can do.

A special profiling application of cross-tabs in statistics packages

You can ask for a special statistic called **adjusted residuals** to appear in cross-tabs in some statistics packages, such as SPSS. Nothing else gives quite as detailed a view of how two scaled variables or nominal variables relate to each other. This goes far beyond the more familiar Chi-square test, which shows only whether the table overall differs significantly from chance. This shows cell-by-cell whether the value is higher or lower than we would expect for that spot in the table.

Figure 13: Adjusted residuals in a cross-tabulation

			6 segments						
			1 Thought-ful	2 Bored	3 Tired	4 With it	5 Wise Ones	6 Shop Til I Drop	Total
	0 t0 4	Count	487	233	248	368	502	735	2573
		% in Segment	25%	16%	7%	42%	23%	32%	21%
		Adjusted Residual	4.3	-5.5	-22.8	15.5	2.6	13.6	
	4 to 7	Count	198	58	51	58	214	237	816
		% in Segment	10%	4%	2%	7%	10%	10%	7%
		Adjusted Residual	6.5	-4.6	-14.0	-.2	6.5	7.4	
Age of child	7 to 10	Count	334	185	106	122	417	402	1566
		% in Segment	17%	13%	3%	14%	19%	17%	13%
		Adjusted Residual	6.0	-.5	-19.6	.9	9.8	6.9	
	11 to 14	Count	542	504	836	205	659	633	3379
		% in Segment	28%	34%	25%	23%	31%	27%	28%
		Adjusted Residual	-.2	5.7	-4.1	-3.1	3.1	-.9	
	15 to 18	Count	392	495	2075	125	359	319	3765
		% inSegment	20%	34%	63%	14%	17%	14%	31%
		Adjusted Residual	-11.5	2.2	45.9	-11.2	-15.9	-20.2	
Total		Count	1953	1475	3316	878	2151	2326	12099
		% inSegment	100%	100%	100%	100%	100%	100%	100%

With this big a sample we can see that even a difference of a few points from the overall average will pass as significant. For instance, in the first row, the percentage of 23% under the Group 5 "Wise Ones" is significantly higher than expected—even though the overall average is just two points lower.

In fact, with this large a sample, we need to look for test values well outside the usual. That is, the test value for 95% significance is +/-1.96. The test value for 90% significance is +/-1.65. You will see good results with smaller samples. This method works very accurately down to about a count of about 10 responses per cell in a table.

You ask for this statistic in SPSS cross-tabs (which itself resides in the "Descriptive Statistics" heading) by choosing the "cell" option in Crosstabs. This very sensitive procedure can turn up differences where standard ways of comparing means or percentages will not.

3. Profiling with discriminant analysis

How this gets done

In segmentation, we would first use the variable identifying the segments as the dependent or grouping variable. This investigation can start with the basis variables and indeed may grow out of diagnosing the segmentation solution.

This might give you part of the descriptive profile that we will discuss later. Profiling could extend to many non-basis variables.

Pros and Cons

If your audience is familiar with discriminant output from diagnosing the segments, this will not require a great deal of explanation. You can set the analysis so that you are reporting on a substantially smaller amount of output than cross-tabs. Like regression, discriminant analysis can be set only to process statistically significant variables. Non-significant variables even might never get out of the analysis into tables, as they do with cross-tabs.
This can be more informative than crosstabs. It quickly pinpoints the variables that most strongly differentiate between segments. As we saw, this method can provide detailed information on how well variables segment the population, and where and in what ways the segments cannot be distinguished. Since it considers all variables simultaneously, you can consider and model interrelations among the variables. Finally, as we saw, it can generate several types of multivariate "perceptual" maps.

The first advantage also shows a possible disadvantage. The output can be difficult for some audiences to interpret , regardless of how clearly you explain it. In the example below, your author learned this lesson on the job. This was chart generally seen as puzzling.

Figure 14: A 3 dimensional map from discriminant analysis

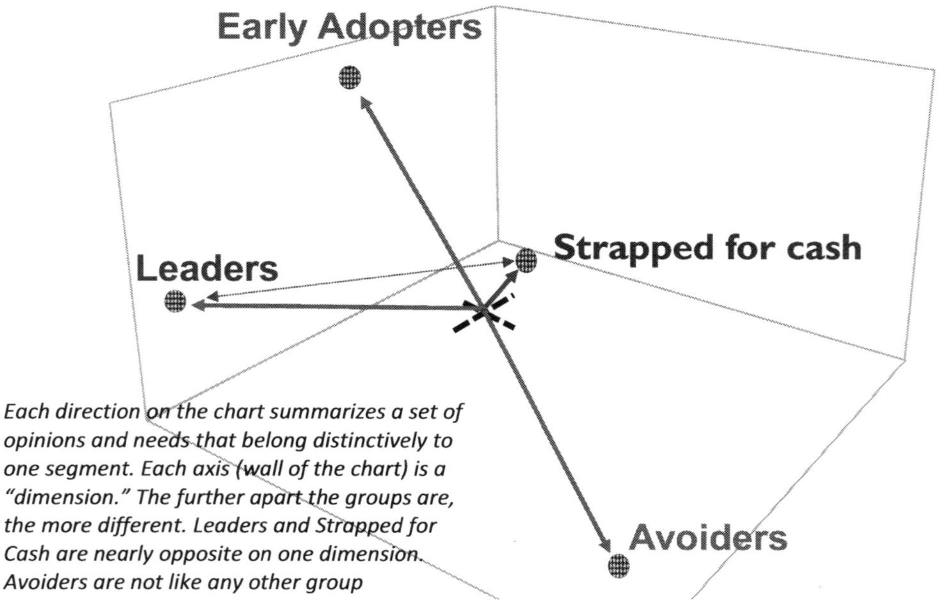
Early Adopters
Strapped for cash
Leaders
Avoiders
Each direction on the chart summarizes a set of opinions and needs that belong distinctively to one segment. Each axis (wall of the chart) is a "dimension." The further apart the groups are, the more different. Leaders and Strapped for Cash are nearly opposite on one dimension. Avoiders are not like any other group

L. Classification Tree Models for Respondent Classification

We talked about classification trees (CHAID, CRT and related programs—the names are numerous)—as a possible means of clustering respondents in Section D. There we mentioned that CHAID has far more usefulness in profiling the segments so they can be **located efficiently.** This is a key step in making segmentation work. This section explains the details.

First, let's review some background on these methods. CHAID quickly gained widespread use in direct marketing, following the highly influential article by Kass (1980). It was immediately apparent that this is a method with great ability to zero in on relatively high incidences of hard-to-find audiences. Advances in CHAID completely overcame the limitations of the older A.I.D. —although some still remained skeptical for many years.

For instance, if an audience is quite rare, say 0.5% of the general population, finding a group where that audience's incidence is 5% raises your odds of locating a member by a factor of ten. Normally, 5% would not sound like very good odd, but if your organization has figured out how to make a living with just a tenth of that, then this was reason to learn something immediately.

One of the most powerful tools arising from classification tree methods is called a **gains analysis** or **leverage analysis**. Starting with a classification tree like the one shown in Section D, the gains analysis adds details and organizes the results. First, here is a complete small tree. Following, we will show how a gains chart emerges from it.

Figure 15: A classification tree with the end nodes numbered

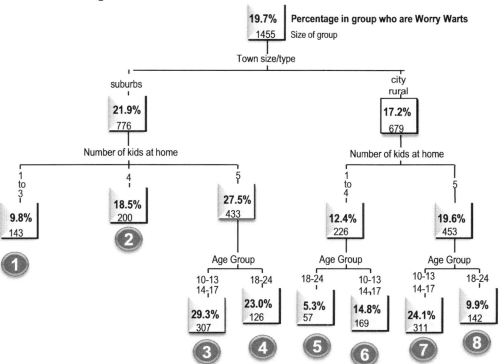

Each spot in the tree is called a **node.** Each node in the tree displays two items of information: the size of the group and the incidence of a target segment, called the Worry Warts. This segment is a target because the product is a pharmaceutical designed to deal with the effects of life's ongoing worries, and as a result they are prime customers.

The tree represents the splitting and re-splitting of the sample

So if we look at the first spot where the tree splits, we can see that the total sample is divided into two groups: those who live in the suburbs vs. a group combining those who live in the cities or rural areas. If we continue downward from there, following to the node below (and where possible) to the one under and the one under, we are following a **branch** in the tree. This tree finally has eight branches, each of which ends in a single node. These terminal nodes are numbered in the diagram.

We can see that the group with the highest incidence of Worry Warts, the node numbered "3," which has 29.3% Worry Warts in it, has a much higher concentration of this segment than the node with the lowest incidence, Node 5. which has only 5.3%. In fact, we are **five times** as likely to encounter a Worry Wart in group represented by Node 3 and we are in the group represented by Node 5.

The characteristics of the group in Node 3 are read as follows: Live in the suburbs AND have 5+ kids at home AND have kids in either the 10 to 13 years or 14 to 17 years of age groups. (No wonder these people worry!)

In Node 5, by way of contrast, people live in cities or rural areas, have 1 to 4 kids at home and have kids only age 18 to 24.

Each place the tree splits, there is a statistically significant difference

Generally we find a very strong contrast between (or among) the groups that are found. For instance, at the top of the tree, the first split is significant at the 0.000001 level or 99.99999% certainty. That is very highly significant.

The program automatically tested all ways of dividing total sample at this juncture. That means it tested all the variables you see here and a lot of others that did not get included in the tree. About 40 variables in total, relating to different demographic characteristics were tested. Some of the variables could be split many ways. For instance, the number of kids could be split into 2 to 5 groups (say 1 vs 2 to 5, 1 or 2 vs. 3 to 5, and so on) in many ways—in fact, this comes out to about 135 different ways this could be split.

We restricted the program's behavior so that splits could take place only with the number of kids remaining in order (so that we could not have a group with 1 kid or 5 kids contrasted with another group having 2, 3, or 4), but this is still many possible splits. The program quickly sorted through them all and found the best possible split (in terms of statistical significance) at that spot. And so it went at all other spots.

The gains chart

This display gives us a way to organize the information in the tree so that it can be used to locate groups in the population with relatively high incidences of the target group, the Worry Warts. Simply, it puts groups in order from highest incidence to lowest incidence, showing the sizes of the groups. It also **cumulates** across groups, showing running averages or totals going down to and including a given group. Let's look at the chart.

Group Characteristics	Group number in the tree diagram	Group size	Group as a % of the total	Incidence of Target Segment	Lift or leverage: Index (100= average)	Groups as a cumulative % of the total	Cumulative Incidence	Cumulative lift or leverage: Index (100= average)
Age Group: 10 -13 and 14-17 AND Number of kids at home: 5 AND Town size/type: suburbs	3	307	21%	29.3%	148.7	21%	29.3%	148.7
Age Group: 10 -13 and 14-17 AND Number of kids at home: 5 ANDTown size/type: city or rural	7	311	21%	24.1%	122.3	42%	26.7%	135.4
Age Group: 18-24 AND Number of kids at home: 5 AND Town size/type: suburbs	4	126	9%	23.0%	116.8	51%	26.1%	132.3
OVERALL STATISTICS		1455	100%	19.7%	100.0			

This is just the top of the gains chart—the first three groups that are highest in incidence of our target segment. These are the groups at the ends of the branches in the tree diagram where we are most likely to find a Worry Wart.

The first group has an incidence of the target segment almost 1.5 times the average, and it makes up 21% of the sample (these figures are circled in Figure 16). If we stopped there, and said this group alone would be our target, we would have some of the Worry Wart population, but likely not enough. Note that the table could also show what percentage of all Worry Warts fall into each group—but for presentation in this format, the table already presents a lot of detail in very small type.

If we add the next group and consider the groups together, we need to look at the **cumulative** numbers. We can see that in adding the next group (node 7 in the diagram), we still would have on average 1.35 times the chance of finding a Worry Wart as we would in the general population. This group is also 21% of the total, or cumulatively across the two groups, we have 42% of the population.

Looking at just these two groups, we have 1.35 times the average odds of finding a Worry Wart, but we are looking at only 42% of the population. So we would be expending less effort than looking at the total population. We gain in efficiency as a result.

In fact, our gain would be 1.35/0.42 or **320% the efficiency of communicating to everybody.**

The model has the strong advantages of being based only easy-to-use demographic characteristics and using only two simple IF—AND style rules. That is, the first rule would run: "IF town size/type is suburban AND number of kids at home is 5+ AND their age groups are 10—13 and 14—17, THEN incidence of Worry Warts is 29.3%." This expresses everything we need to find this group without any equations.

This type of chart is where segmentation becomes highly useful. We have a group that we understand and we know where we are most likely to find it in a straightforward fashion. An analysis like this one supplies the final component that can bring a segmentation study from hard work to insight and finally to action.

Other analyses using logistic regression also have been used in a similar way. Rather than IF—AND rules, these use complex equations and calculate odds. CHAID analyses also can form a starting point for this type of a logistic regression model, pointing out **interactions**.

M. Descriptive Profiling

Describing or **profiling** the segments is key to making effective use of a segmentation study . We have addressed describing segments to an extent in earlier sections. However, there is a very wide range of methods and approaches you can use to convey the nature of the segments—and finally to bring them to life for your audience.

These methods can involve charting, graphing and narratives. Pictures, and in some cases even videos, have been used to supplement the basic findings. Videos can be made, for instance, by locating people very representative of each segment and filming them in action. Getting the right people for filming requires use of a scoring model (as we discussed in Section I part 3) and some perseverance. However, where this has been done, it typically captures the attention of those in the executive quarters. They may actually put away their devices and watch—and listen.

We do not have film clips here, but will run through the basic forms of profiling. These include the following:

- pie charts with group names
- narratives about members of one group
- numeric summaries of group characteristics for one group
- visual summaries of group differences and similarities
- maps showing importances and ratings within a segment
- maps comparing segments
- other visual summaries.

Group names and pie charts

Perhaps the easiest-to-digest output arising from the work you do profiling is the naming of the segments. This may take time and involve a great deal of discussion, and likely will undergo a change or two. The final names typically appear along with a pie chart showing the relative sizes of the segments (as long as the pie does not use fake 3-D and distort the proportions). A display like this seems to appear in the report for every segmentation study.

Figure 17: A pie chart with segment names

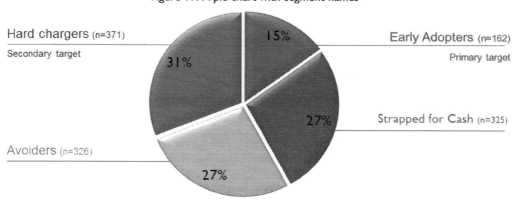

Hard chargers (n=371)
Secondary target
31%

Early Adopters (n=162)
Primary target
15%

Strapped for Cash (n=325)
27%

Avoiders (n=326)
27%

Narratives about members of one segment

These stories describe without numbers and give an overall portrayal of a segment's members. This one is augmented by a fine picture showing a highly representative group member.

Figure 18: Narrative description of one segment

Doctors in the "Aggressive treatment" segment

- An excellent audience if you can convince them of the value of the product
  - Most are in the sixth to ninth deciles in volume and have high Rx shares for our product
  - Particularly interested in Rx having low levels of somnolence and relapse
- Opinion leaders.
  - Speak at conferences; peers often ask them for advice
- Engaged and not averse to challenges
  - Confident about their ability to take care of patients, including titrating medications and dealing with side effects
- See more difficult patients than other doctors
- Somewhat impatient with detailing efforts
- Seek better patient information and better staff information

Numeric summaries of group characteristics for one group

This chart lays out the strongest positive and negative opinions of a group. Although it is quite small in this format, we can still see that it quickly conveys what is most distinctive about this group. The bars in the chart show differences from the overall average.

Figure 19: Numeric summary for one group

"Strapped for cash" segment

Rating scale is 1.0 (negative) to 5.0 (positive) unless otherwise noted.	Gap of Mean vs. Total		Mean
	Lesser Association ◄ ► Greater Association		
Never seem to have enough to pay all basic expenses		0.8	3.5
Cannot afford individual life insurance know I need		0.7	3.6
Concerned my family will not have enough money for future		0.6	4.2
Selecting individual life insurance is confusing		0.6	3.9
Wish I had more individual life insurance coverage		0.5	4.1
Hard to find people you can trust re financial matters		0.4	4.2
Wish were easier to get info for making individual life ins. decisions		0.3	3.9
When it comes to financial matters not sophisticated		0.3	3.0
Once buy individual life ins never want to think about it again		0.3	3.6
Look for ways to save money when shopping		0.2	4.6
Too much info out there to compare financial choices thoroughly		0.2	3.1
Try to have as much information as possible when make a decision		0.2	4.5
Likely to purchase life insurance in this manner	-0.4		2.0
Find believable a co. could offer life ins. as described and do it well	-0.4		2.6
Comfortable only dealing with an agent online	-0.5		2.0
Would purchase life ins. from a co. who sent me unsolicited email	-0.5		1.7
Save money for unexpected events	-0.5		3.1
Much better off financially than 5 years ago	-0.5		2.9
Would look into life ins. from a co. who sent me unsolicited email	-0.6		1.9
Feel I control my financial situation	-0.6		2.8

-1.5   -1.0   -0.5   0.0   0.5   1.0   1.5
Negative ← Gap Rating Scale → Positive

Visual summary for several groups

This dispenses with numbers and uses simple graphics to compare and contrast.

Figure 20: Summary for several groups

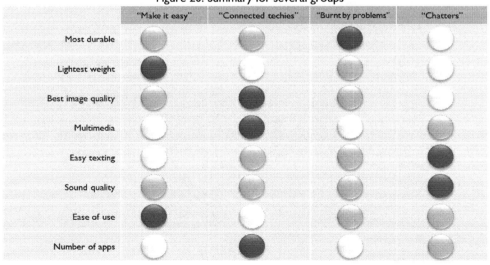

	"Make it easy"	"Connected techies"	"Burnt by problems"	"Chatters"
Most durable				
Lightest weight				
Best image quality				
Multimedia				
Easy texting				
Sound quality				
Ease of use				
Number of apps				

● Significantly higher importance than other segments   ○ Significantly lower importance than other segments
◐ Average

90

Maps showing details about one segment

This type of map is a mainstay of reporting inside and outside segmentation studies. One axis (usually the horizontal) shows how important respondents found each attribute. The other axis shows how well a brand or organization was rated on those same attributes.

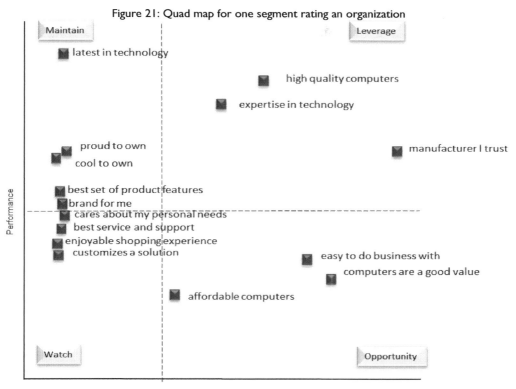

Figure 21: Quad map for one segment rating an organization

The typical practice, observed here, divides this maps into four regions or quadrants, hence the name **quad map**. The names that are applied to the quadrants come from judgment and other similar names have been used. The idea is that areas of high importance and low performance need immediate attention, which in typically optimistic fashion is called "opportunity." High performance and high importance attributes are salient strengths and can be used to support the brand in communications. The ideas behind the remaining quadrants should be similarly clear. High performance and low importance together imply areas that can be left as they are. Low importance and low performance is the area that matter least, but this is rightfully labeled "Watch."

You will notice that importance is **derived,** as stated in the label on the axis. That is, the survey wisely did not trust respondents to rate directly how important they found each attribute. Rather, a model was constructed, linking these attributes to an overall rating, and the strengths of these attributes in influencing that rating was determined.

The map uses averages to devise the quadrants: half above and half below on each dimension. This is a convention, but arbitrary—other ways of dividing up the points are possible.

Maps comparing segments (perceptual or multivariate maps)

These maps are typically based on **correspondence analysis**, and sometimes related methods called **bi-plots** and **MD-PREF**. We discussed correspondence analysis in Section E, as occasionally used to develop segments. We also mentioned the idea that these maps are used far more often as displays for comparing segments.; showing how segments compare and contrast across many areas.

As a reminder, in this type of map, groups fall closest to those attributes that they rated most highly or which were most important to them. The input for this map is a table, typically with the segments as columns and the ratings or importances (or consumption levels) in the rows. Only this summary data is used, and the patterns are translated into distances in an x-y map.

Distance from the center of the map (the area inside the dotted circle) also has meaning. Attributes that fall in the center do not differentiate among the groups and groups that fall in the center do not have any distinctive ratings. In this map, the Avoiders group expressed no strong needs. This pattern of not caring about anything related to the topic strongly contributed to the name given to this group.

Figure 22: Correspondence map comparing segments

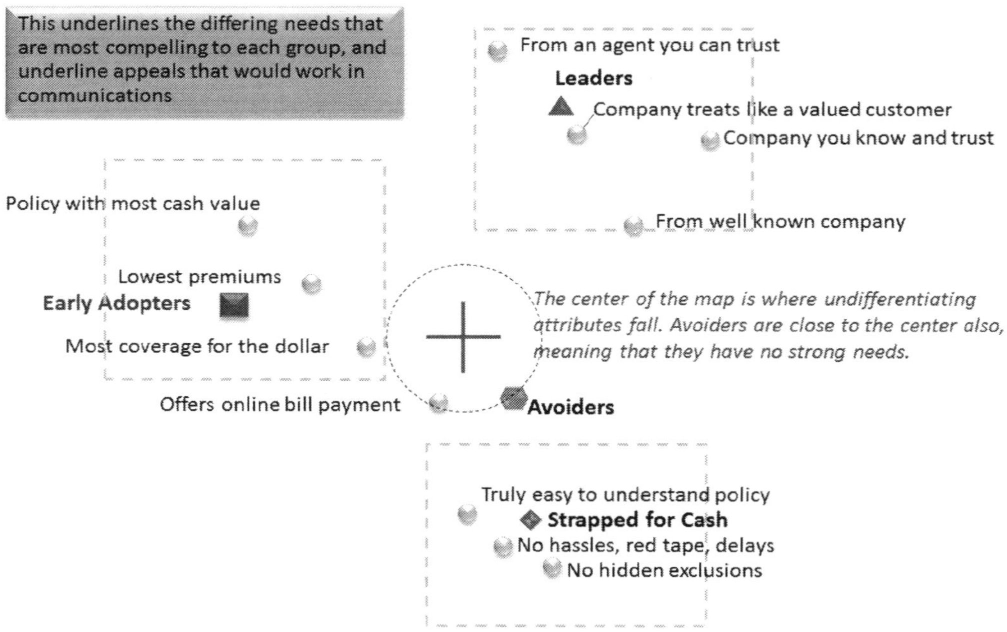

In a report or presentation, a map at full size (and in color) can provide a highly compelling visual summary of complex tabulated information. Typically, organizations with more marketing experience find maps like these invaluable. Less sophisticated viewers may find them somewhat difficult to understand.

The gains chart

As the narrative above the chart summarizes, this can play a key role in making the results of the study usable. Without this or a similar analysis, locating target segments efficiently can be difficult or impossible.

Other types of scoring models, particularly those built using logistic regression, have also been widely used. Logistic-regression based models use equations and calculate the odds that a person belongs to the target segment. Although the modeling is more complex, the outcome is similar: everybody to whom the model is applied (typically in a database of some sort) is given a likelihood of belonging to the target segment. Marketing efforts are extended only to those with the strongest likelihood of belonging to the target segment.

Finding groups where prospects are prevalent, while avoiding those who are very unlikely to be in the target group, gives the model its efficiency.

Figure 23: Sample gains chart

- This is where segmentation finally pays off with efficient results
- A precise "road map" showing how to reach target segment members efficiently, based on demographics and media usage—characteristics that can "tag" prospects in data files. Uses simple "AND" combinations—no equations, so easy to program into databases
- Output from classification tree analysis, with segment membership as the target variable

Group Characteristics: Five top groups based on demographics and readership	Group as a pct. of Total	Incidence of Segment	Lift or Leverage: Index(100 = average)	Cumulative % of Total	Cumulative incidence of Segment	Cumulative Lift or Leverage
1 Industry: Personal services, FIRE AND Refer to regularly: iii Website: YES AND Subscribe: Insurance and Technology: NO AND Number of employees: 5 to 24	6%	61%	362	6%	61%	362
2 Subscribe: Insurance Chronicle: YES AND Number of employees: 5 to 24	4%	60%	355	10%	61%	359
3 Subscribe: Insurance and Technology: YES AND Refer to regularly: iii Website: No AND Subscribe: Insurance Chronicle: NO AND Number of employees: 5 to 24	5%	36%	211	15%	53%	313
4 Refer to regularly: iii Website: YES AND Subscribe: Insurance and Technology: NO AND Number of employees: 25-49	4%	26%	153	19%	47%	276
5 Subscribe: Insurance and Technology: YES AND Number of employees: 25-49	9%	25%	145	28%	40%	235

Cumulative improvement in efficiency
vs. no model =
2.35 (boost in incidence)/**0.28**
(due to avoiding lower incidence groups)=
840% the efficiency of not having this model

This is only the topmost part of the whole chart—later groups failing lower in the would be those where likelihood of finding the target market is relatively low. These are groups to be ignored—and in the case of those with the lowest incidences, avoided.

Pictorial summary of groups' similarities and differences

Displays of information from segmentation studies are limited only by needs to convey information and your imagination.

This is a pictorial summary of two separate analyses that lays things out so simply even those in the boardroom are likely to follow. Note that this was made from questions often not part of segmentation studies about leisure activities that were added to the descriptor variables. This was intended to add depth to the portrayals of the groups. Careful consideration of your audience will determine whether imaginative displays like this have extra value.

The key question always remains: Does this communicate in a way that is meaningful and can lead to action? Displays need to gain attention and make it easy for audiences to see the key points —and so act upon what they a re seeing.

Figure 24: An imaginative pictorial summary

Results of two classification tree (CHAID) analyses are merged into a single pictorial summary

Segment 4 "Pro Users" | Segment 2 "Brand Believers"

Distinguishing characteristics

✓ Shop at Cabela's retail store
✓ Politics
✓ Hunting/shooting

✓ Visit news websites regularly
✓ Bible/devotional/church
✓ Fitness/exercise

Similar characteristics

✓ Shop at Bass Pro Shops retail store
✓ Shop online
✓ Family
✓ DIY

94

N. Fuzzy Classification

Fuzzy classification or clustering is a worthwhile method that gets less use than it deserves. The idea behind it is that respondents are not classified into clusters, but instead are given scores representing their likelihood of belonging to each of the clusters. Moving from this likelihood to a definite cluster assignment is quite simple, though, as we just pick the group where the score is highest. However, the extra information we find in fuzzy clustering can be highly informative.

As we saw in the section on discriminant analysis where we discussed respondent-by-respondent classification statistics, almost no respondent has a 100% fit with any given segment. Therefore we can think of all clustering as being inherently fuzzy, and so we can gain considerable understanding by seeing respondents' odds of belonging to the various segments.

Below we have some technical-looking output from a fuzzy clustering program. For purposes of understanding fit in a group, the "P(G/D)" column (or the **posterior probability**) provides highly valuable information. For Case 1, this says that we would give this case a 59.6% probability of belonging to group 3. (Group 3 is the highest group, the one in which discriminant analysis would predict Case 1 to belong.) In addition, discriminant analysis gives this person a 26.6% probability of belonging to group 2, the next highest group.

Case #	Highest probability group	P(G/D)	2nd highest	P(G/D)	Discriminant Scores				
1	3	0.5964	2	0.2659	-1.52	0.723	3.1945	-0.817	1.8306
2	1	0.6614	2	0.2091	0.178	-1.131	1.433	-1.299	0.717
3	2	0.3173	1	0.2715	-1.94	-0.029	0.8322	2.2642	1.624
4	3	0.2628	1	0.2589	-0.09	1.4031	0.8759	0.4813	-0.122

This information has particular value if you want to analyze only respondents who typify or epitomize a segment. To do this, you may exclude from some analyses any respondents who do not have a strong probability of belonging to any cluster. Many other forms of analysis are possible with this information. For instance, you might compare the profiles of respondents with higher and lower probabilities of belonging to a given cluster.

Alternatively, you might wish to profile those respondents who discriminant analysis identified as misclassified, to see how they differ from correctly classified respondents. You also could run another discriminant analysis within a cluster group, comparing the correctly classified and misclassified respondents, and so on. Analyzing likelihood of belonging to a group can provide many useful insights into the nature of segments.

O. Clustering Using the Q-Method: A Discredited Method

Basics

Just as we discussed the appropriate methods of segmentation, we also need to discuss on method that should not be used so that you can be prepared if you ever encounter it.

Q-type factor analysis tries to group respondents as the more usual factor analysis (technically called the **R-factor** variety) tries to group variables. While Q - Type factor analysis has little to justify its continued use in clustering, you will still see it from time to time. This section will help familiarize you with this procedure's basic aims, in case you come across it. Q-factoring also is part of a larger method that includes **Q-sorting**. This form of sorting is just a guided partial ranking of items (only the most favored and least favored items are ranked, usually top 3 in order within a broader group of the top 10, and the bottom 3 ordered within a broader group of the bottom 10). This ranking can lead to very clear relative likings or importances for very long lists of items. Success with up to 100 items has been reported in the literature. However, this does not make the clustering routine added to this sorting any less invalid.

Objectives

The goals sound much like the goals for any clustering exercise. However, the assumptions and mathematics behind the procedure remain highly questionable. Goals would include:

- ♦ To reduce many subjects to a smaller set of groups (segments), called "factors," by using factor-style combinations of the subjects' responses to the basis variables;

- ♦ to examine the nature and strength of the relationships within groups;

- ♦ to assess the amount of variability between segments;

- ♦ to determine the position of each subject group in the factor space, using factor scores.

Critical assumptions and problems

The models used to reduce the data structure are primarily based on linear relationships among the subjects' responses to the basis variables. The decision on how many factors (that is, segments) to keep depends largely on judgment. So does the interpretation of the factors (segments).

Particularly problematic, for analyzing people, is the meaning of the pure types or factors to which this procedure reduces individuals. Similarly, possible meanings of individuals' "loadings" into these pure types remains unclear. Recall that factor analysis **reduces data.** In a questionnaire given to individual respondents, we can easily understand that certain questions have some redundancy, and so can be reduced or combined. (This corresponds to the more usual R-type analysis.) Q-Factor analysis more closely aligns with idea of reducing people while assuming the questions need no reduction.

The use of Q-Type factor analysis has met with severe criticism in the literature over the years. Stewart (1981) identified this as one of the primary abuses of the factor analytic technique in his article "The Application and Misapplication of Factor Analysis in Marketing Research." There appears to be little theoretical or practical support for Q-Type factors analysis as a workable way of classifying subjects into groups. Q-Factoring is not normally appropriate for segmenting a market.

P. When Segmentation Produces Poor Results

Suppose that you still get poor results after you run the diagnostics suggested in the last few sections, and you run several types of clustering, comparing each. This will be highly unlikely after the steps that we have suggested, but it is best to be prepared.

1. Examine the most likely spots for unexpected errors

Let's take a minute to review some of the ways that extra error can work its way into a study. Some authors call extra error "unexplained variance," but here those words actually mean the same thing. We cannot cover all possible sources, as there are far more ways to make mistakes than to do things well. Some possible sources, though, might include:

A. Too few basis variables OR too much heterogeneity in these variables

Since too few variables and too many types of variables can both produce poor results, you need to strike a balance. As a reminder, if you first tried the clustering based on opinions and attitudinal statements, then your best option is including questions related to product usage. However, adding widely diverse types of questions (for instance, combining attitudes, perceptions, importance ratings, usage and demographics) may leave you with too much—so that nothing emerges as distinctive among the many concerns covered.

These considerations suggest that segmentation studies have better odds of succeeding if they provide several medium-to-long batteries of questions that approach key issues, understanding that these may include all the items listed—except demographics—among the basis variables. Including one battery of attitudinal items and one battery of usage related items seems a minimum for a successful study. If the questionnaire design does not allow for an adequate set of basis variables, you may well find yourself in an intractable position. See section 4 below for a suggestion on what to do.

B. Biased or inappropriate questions

Some questions have a much lower likelihood than others of working. If your questionnaire includes these, you can try to remove them from the basis set. Look carefully to see if any might confuse a respondent. "No answer" levels can provide a clue. Even in mainly sound questionnaires, you may find a question will not match well with the responses available.

One problem area we have encountered too often is a question using a qualifier , such as "sometimes" (or "occasionally," or "generally") with a and agreement scale. Such scales might range from (for instance) "disagree strongly" to "agree strongly." For example, consider this questionnaire item: "I occasionally like to look for bargains." Respondents who *always* look for bargains and those who *never* look would both disagree with this item.

Questions phrased more positively, with "usually," or "mostly" may fare little better with scaled answers. Dropping such items from the basis variables can improve results.

Remember that clustering can show great sensitivity to anomalies in the data. Any questions that respondents find hard to answer can produce such anomalies.

C. Random variation in the sample

Few cures for this exist, other than trying to exclude respondents who do not belong in the sample population (as section 3 below discusses). If you have missed respondents you needed, then you may have to re-field the study, or suffer mightily when this comes to light.

Please do NOT assume that, because you are using an online panel, responses will match your audience in all important ways. For instance, suppose you have stores in all 50 states and that it is therefore critical to have at least some sample from each. You cannot expect the online panel to get this for you unless you explicitly set quotas by state. Not long ago, for instance, one researcher simply said he wanted a national sample of mothers with children of certain ages. After thousands of interviews were completed, the organization was quite dismayed to discover than about 30% came from California and only 15 states were represented at all.

This could have been avoided by setting state quotas, rather than assuming it would all wash out in a big enough sample. The sample should have been **released** slowly and progress continuously monitored. If many respondents are invited to participate at one time, answers may show up from the coastal regions earlier.

2. Try yet another algorithm

You should as a rule try more than one algorithm for clustering. If you use SPSS, you can find online syntax examples that show how to do seeding of K-means, for instance. Also, there are free programs such as R, Rapid Miner and Weka that include different clustering algorithms. As a reminder, all methods show "preferences" for certain patterns in the data. If you used K-means and Ward's method, try TwoStep in SPSS or a complete linkage method, and so on. Where one fails, the other often succeeds.

3. Drop atypical respondents

You need to take extra care with a segmentation study. It of course should go without saying that all studies require great care. Still, "outliers" (respondents with truly strange responses) and even unusual cases can ruin a segmentation scheme that would otherwise work well. Try dropping respondents who do not fit well into any of the larger clusters.

Most frustratingly, atypical respondents sometimes will fall into small "splinter" clusters of 1 to 10 or so. Methods such as Complete Linkage and Ward's methods appear particularly prone to forming splinters. If you keep atypical respondents in the data, you may have to generate solutions with large numbers of clusters (20 or more in some cases) to get more than one large cluster and splinters.

Fortunately, there is a very handy method for detecting outliers. This is a method of plotting variables called (in terminology that once again is rather tone deaf), the **box plot** or the **box and whisker** plot. This is based on computations starting with the **median**—an average in the sense that half the values are above it and half the values are below it. Below we have some output from SPSS after requesting a box plot. You will notice that the program provides case numbers or locations in the file for specific individuals whose answers are extreme.

If you encounter **outlier** responses, you can deal with the individuals responsible either by eliminating them from the analysis entirely or by **rolling back** their responses to more reasonable values. This rolling back means simply substituting a value at the edge of the expected distribution (shown by the whisker on the graph) for a more extreme value. This is a well-accepted procedure and if you do this with a large group of respondents with extreme responses, it has a name: **winsorising.**

Figure 25: A box plot and how it detects outliers

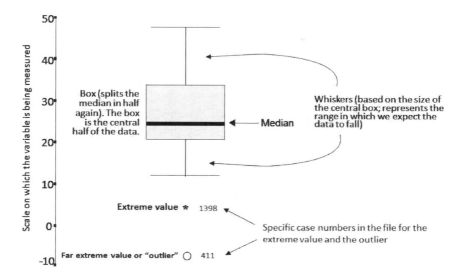

4. If all else fails. . .

You might unwisely conclude that you cannot segment the market, as you view it. However, most organizations will not receive this with great enthusiasm. Professor S. Hunt, not too seriously, once suggested a solution to this dilemma. Since even a relatively serious overview book like this can make **one passing stab at a joke**, we will send this along:

"No matter what happens, always have a plan."

Therefore, if you find no segments, simply find the next best substitute and proceed as if you did. Assuming nobody is hyper-vigilant, by the time anybody figures out the truth, you will have been promoted for having a plan—or better yet, you will have departed for a more enlightened organization. It will then become somebody else's problem.

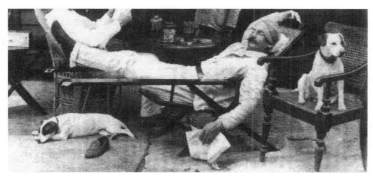

Q. Putting the Results to Work

Once the statistical analysis has ended, and once all the charts are completed, we are not, to use a well-worn phrase, out of the woods. You still faces some stiff challenges:

⇒ Assembling everything into a coherent narrative interpreting the results,

⇒ Understanding the marketing implications, and

⇒ Conveying those to the client, whether internal or external.

Is there light at the end of the forest?

How this happens depends on the organization. We have given you some examples of output that has been helpful in many studies, Unfortunately, we could give you many more examples, seen in person, of output that has not helped or even hurt.

While there are no absolutes, here as elsewhere, some of critical preliminary questions and essential elements in communication follow, to complete the sequence. These are some key hurdles to clear:

☞ Do the segments, in general outline, pass the test of common sense?[1] If not, why not? How can you explain any surprises in your findings? If nothing surprises you, what are the reasons for this, and what did you get out of the study?

Experience has taught us to suspect both too many and too few surprises

☞ Can you convey the segments easily to people not that familiar with the study, such as senior management

☞ Can promotional, communications, and product differentiation strategies successfully approach these segments?

☞ How can findings effectively translate into a strategy, and help guide tactics in support of that strategy?

[1] Here somebody is may raise his voice to point out that Galileo's observations did not make sense in and about 1615, but aside from the fact that the implied comparison seems just a little presumptuous, the issues are not the same. Here we are talking about having an underlying sense of behaviors and responses in a specific setting, not the answers to a large cosmological question.

R. In Conclusion

Market segmentation can serve as a powerful marketing tool. In any country where you are likely to offer your product, service or non-profit organization, there would be little to no chance to thrive without a strategy involving market segmentation.

Segmenting a market properly can improve marketing, distribution, and manufacturing efficiency. This in turn can generate additional sales, enrollments, contributions, memberships or subscriptions—and so market share and cash on hand. Although the world of Big Data is upon us, true segmentation will always provide an advantage. Big Data at its root comes down to collecting as much as is possible, trying to clean up what you have, linking it correctly, and then asking intelligent questions. (We are best off ignoring the frequent claims that having a lot of "stuff" can magically provide all answers—as much of this stuff often is the digital equivalent of random noise). As probing as we may be about what we have on hand, **original research** remains the best way to strike out in new directions for the future. At its core, segmentation is about taking those new directions.

The basis variables selected for segmenting a market remain key. The effective application of well-considered basis variables can provide a strategic advantage to the innovative organization. Including category-related behaviors in this critical set, while not skimping on perceptions and needs, greatly boosts the odds of the segmentation scheme you develop being effective.

A strategy of market segmentation must gain support at the very top of the organization, and must permeate the organization. If an organization takes segmentation seriously, it will affect its audiences, its products and/or services, and the appeals it makes. Collaboration is critical.

Market segmentation research must use the highest professional research standards of planning and execution. Segmenting a market incorrectly arguably is no better than treating the market as one undifferentiated mass, and might even do harm. While the excuse that a poorly crafted study "is better than nothing" may buy some forgiveness in certain settings, segmentation is one situation in which doing a poor job can do lasting damage.

If a firm can address its markets via a new vision of how that market operates, uncovering the needs and wants of the market's segments, it often has opportunities to act that will elude its competition. It is no secret that a number of successful foreign firms have entered the U.S. marketplace by segmenting the market, uncovering an underserved niche, and concentrating their marketing and financial resources upon that segment.

It is also worth recalling that segmentation works by increasing the probability of making a correct decision. It does not provide certain answers. No method yet devised, or likely to be devised, can reveal the ultimate truth about a market. All procedures for uncovering segments have salient limitations. Intelligent and effective application of these methods requires an understanding of both their strengths and weaknesses.

These methods, in sum, can do a great deal to improve your effectiveness in dealing with your market. If we can end with an appeal to thought, when easy answers seem to retain all their perennial appeal, these approaches will always do the most when applied with careful consideration and judgment.

Part V
Step-by Step though a Market Segmentation Study

Because segmentation is so complex and multifaceted, there is no one absolutely correct way to do it, but generally these steps need to get done.

1. Start by **meeting and talking** with all of those who will need to work with the segmentation results or who will be strongly influenced by them—or as it is often put, the stakeholders. It is critical at this stage to get a firm grasp of their needs, problems and ideas (often including questions they really want in the questionnaire).

2. **Write the questionnaire**. This is a very complex undertaking and putting it this way is a little like the do-it-yourself column which starts its instructions for a project by saying, "First remove the roof of the house and put it to one side." This step entails thinking of all the possible basis and descriptor variables. Please look back at the section on **preferred bases for segmentation** to get an idea of how many objectives segmentation might address. Typically this step also involves a great deal of discussion. Areas will expand and more rarely contract. The first drafts usually are too long. Sometimes these run 45 minutes, 60 minutes or longer. This is too long, even when you compensate study participants. Expect that you can hold them for 25 or maybe 30 minutes if the survey is very interesting to them.

3. **Collect, clean and correct the data**. As a reminder, clustering is one form of analysis that is particularly prone to disaster when extreme results or **outliers** get into the mix. Also, pay close attention to missing values. Most clustering routines drop respondents who have more than a few missing values, and some routines will drop a respondent with one missing response. How you fill the missing data is critical. Just plugging in an average value rarely works well. Sometimes you really need to think about what missing data means—for instance, if only product users get to say how much they know about a product, all non-users should be forced into the code that corresponds to "never used" (usually at the low end of the scale on this question), not recoded to the average value.

4. **Analyze patterns in candidate basis variables** and reduce their numbers. Methods could include exploratory factor analysis, categorical principal components analysis or various modeling methods, such as **random forests**, which develop variable importances.

5. **Group the respondents**. You boost the odds of a successful study greatly by trying many alternative methods of clustering or grouping the variables. There are any number of ways to do this, including traditional linkage methods and a multitude of iterative K-means approaches. Any of these might work well if the variables are all continuous or scalar. If have categorical variables are in the mix, consider any of a number of alternatives, such as latent class analysis, fuzzy clustering, TwoStep clustering, and EM clustering.

6. **Diagnose the best candidate solutions**. Methods such as discriminant analysis and multinomial logit point out the similarities and differences among the groups and lead to fuller understanding of the solution. Data display methods, allowing you to examine the data (such as the SPSS AIM procedure) also can provide additional insights.

7. **Uncover key distinctions**. Determine which variables differentiate most strongly and meaningfully. Prepare charts and map key distinctions. Discriminant analysis and correspondence analysis (and related methods such as bi-plots and MDPREF) can be highly useful in revealing patterns in the data.

8. **Name the groups**. Here is a good time to have another general discussion or brainstorming session. Although it is tempting to do naming right away, it works better to have place-holder names until a clear picture of the groups, and what makes them distinctive, emerges. Sometimes these sessions run a long time—and one or two even generated some strong emotions. To the right you will see a record of part of a naming session done with help of a whiteboard.

9. **Locate the target audience or audiences efficiently**. Methods that have had long and successful use in direct mail and CRM work exceptionally well with segmentation, providing the needed way to reach these audiences selectively and efficiently. Precisely locating best targets audiences entails a gains or lift analysis, as we discussed. It powerfully combines well-established analytical methods in specific ways to give the strongest results for efficiently locating target audiences and for developing scoring models to describe the segments.

10. **Develop classification models for later use.** These usually would be done using classification trees or by generating equations using discriminant analysis on the basis variables. Record the classification function coefficients or classification tree model for use in later studies to classify respondents into the same segments.

11. **Conduct any follow-up qualitative or ethnographic research** needed to add depth and detail to the segments. Doing this starts with a scoring model that gives the likelihood of a respondent belonging to each segment. This way, people recruited for follow-up work can be restricted to only those who are very representative of their segment. We have found that anybody with about an 80% to 85% chance (or more) of belonging to one segment will typically express opinions and have behaviors typical of that segment.

*Highly typical segment members (these are **stylish, practical** and **disinterested** shoppers) can be found via use of a scoring model. Integrating snippets about representative people can help the study come to life.*

An annotated (and abridged) segmentation questionnaire

Tool segmentation: Questionnaire (online)

Qualified re-spondent	Is an adult (18 or older) who lives in the US	S1=2 & S2 GE 18
	Lives in a household that passes screening for sensitive/competitive employment	S3_3=1
	Is a decision-maker for outdoor gear and...	S4=1 OR 2
	Has purchased a tool for themselves in the past 12 months or	STATUS=1
	received (as a gift) a tool in the past 12 months AND uses their tool at least "once in a while" or	STATUS=2
	Has purchased a tool for someone else in the past 12 months	STATUS=3
Sample size goal	N=500	
Sample source (s)/ strategy	Online panel supplemented with targeted sample lists	
Quotas/quota controls	Tool users (n=575 with final target of 500) split among...	
	Maximum 50% Leatherhead-branded users (maximum n=287)	S7=2
	Minimum 15% (n=86) and maximum 20% (n=115) buyers who are not end-users—that is, gift givers	STATUS=2

Programmer instructions

Timing information to be collected

Thank you for agreeing to take this survey about outdoor gear. Please be as detailed as you can, and please try to make your answers complete. Remember, there are no wrong answers to any of our questions.

The survey should take about 20 minutes to complete.

During the survey, please do not use your browser's FORWARD or BACK buttons. Instead, always use the "Continue" button at the bottom of the screen to move forward through the survey.

Screening questions

S1 In what country or region of the world do you <u>currently</u> live?
Please select only one.
Canada 1
United States 2
Central/South America 3
Australia 4
Asia 5
Europe 6
Africa/Middle East 7
Somewhere else 8

> These questions decide who gets into the survey. Anything in brackets and/or all upper case letters would be instructions that the respondent does not get to see.

S2 What is your age, please?

Please enter your response as a whole number (without decimal points) in the space below.
_1 Your age (in years): **[ANSWER BOX: ALLOW NUMERIC RESPONSES BETWEEN 1 & 99]**
_2 Would rather not say

S3 Do you, or does any member of your household, work for any of the following?
Please select all that apply.
_1 An advertising, public relations or market research firm 1
_2 A periodical or other media organization that covers the outdoor equipment industry 2
_3 None of these 3

> People in these industries usually do not get to participate in surveys—either lucky or not depending on your views.

[DO NOT ALLOW THE CHOICE OF S3_3 ALONG WITH ANY OTHER S3 RESPONSES]
[IF S1 NE 2 *(R does not live in the US)*, CODE DISPO=21 & TERMINATE]
[IF S2_2=1 *(R is unwilling to divulge his/her age)*, CODE DISPO=2 & TERMINATE]

[IF S2_1 LE 17 *(R is younger than 18)*, CODE DISPO=22 & TERMINATE]
[IF S3_3 NE 1 *(R or one of R's household members works in a sensitive/non-secure field/ industry)*, CODE DISPO=23 & TERMINATE]

S4   Which of the following statements best describes your decision-making role when it comes to the purchase of outdoor gear or tools for your own personal use?
Please select only one.

I am the sole decision-maker when it comes to deciding which outdoor gear or tools are purchased for my personal use	1
I share this responsibility with another person or persons	2
I never get involved in the decision-making behind such purchases	3

[IF S4=3 *(R does not have adequate decision-making responsibility)*, CODE DISPO=24 & TER-MINATE] [IF S4=1 OR 2, ASK S5]

S5   Which of the following products —if any—have **you purchased or received** (as a gift) in the past year—**since August 20XX?**

Purchased after August 20XX	Received (as a gift) after August 20XX
_1	_2

Please select only one.
[RANDOMIZE PRESENTATION ORDER OF LIST ITEMS 1–11]
_1   Any type of axe or hatchet
_2   Any type of tool
_3   Any type of kayak
_4   Any type of sporting knife (for example, a hunting knife)
_5   Any type of camping tent
_6   Any type of shotgun
_7   Any type of headlamp
_8   Any type of binoculars
_9   Any type of flashlight
_10   Any type of fishing equipment (for example, poles, lures)
_11   Any type of compass
_12   Any type of handgun

[IF S5_1_2 NE 1 OR S5_2_2 NE 1 *(R has neither purchased nor received a tool since August 2005)*, CODE DISPO=25 & TERMINATE]
[IF S5_1_2=1 OR S5_2_2=1, ASK S7]

S6   [NOT USED]

> As questionnaires change, some items may drop out at the last minute.

S7   What brand of tool did you most recently acquire?

Please select only one. If you have acquired more than 1 tool since August 20XX, se-lect the brand you acquired most recently.
[RANDOMIZE PRESENTATION ORDER OF LIST ITEMS 1–5]

Sparky   1
Leatherhead   2
Trojan Army   3
London Tower   4
Crafty   5
Some other tool brand, please specify **[FORCE IF SELECTED]**   6
Don't know   7

[IF S7=7 *(R doesn't know the tool brand they acquired)*, CODE DISPO=2 & TERMINATE] [IF S7 NE 7 ASK S8]

S8   How did you acquire the **[PIPE: S7]** tool?

I purchased it using personal or household funds for my own use   1

I purchased it using personal or household funds for someone else—a gift   2

I received it as a gift from someone   3

My work gave it to me for my work-related purposes 4

I acquired it through some other circumstances   5

> **Pipe** means pull up the answer given earlier

[IF S8 GE 4 *(R was issued a tool via non-applicable means)*, CODE DISPO=27 & TERMINATE]
[IF S8=2 *(R is a tool giver)*, SKIP TO "CREATE NEW VARIABLE: STATUS"]
[IF S8=1 OR 3, ASK S9]

S9   How often do you use your **[PIPE: S7]** tool?
       Please select only one.

Never   1
Once in a while   2
Often   3

[If s8=3 & s9=1 *(R received tool as a gift but doesn't use it)*, code dispo=28 & terminate]

[Status of tool respondent.]

[IF S8=1 & S9=1)] Tool purchaser, non-user 1
[IF (S8=1 OR S8=3) & S9 GE 2)] Tool user   2
[IF S8=2] Tool giver   3

[Sample disposition code assignment.]

R met all the screening criteria   1
R refused to answer a question required for screening   2
DQ: R lives outside the US   21
DQ: R is younger than 18   22

DQ:	R lives in a household that failed the employment screen	23	
DQ:	R does not have adequate decision-making responsibility	24	We have finally
DQ:	R has neither purchased nor received a tool since Aug.	25	concluded who
DQ:	R acquired a tool more than 1 year ago	26	gets into the sur-
DQ:	R was issued a tool via non-applicable means	27	vey and in which
DQ:	R, a gift receiver, has inadequate usage to qualify	28	group.
OQ:	Over quota for Leatherhead users/givers	51	
OQ:	Over quota for tool givers	52	

Acquisition process

Q1   **[SHOW IF S8=3]** Who gave you the **[PIPE: S7]** tool?
[SHOW IF S8=1 OR 2] Who did you purchase the **[PIPE: S7]** tool for...?
Please select only one.
My spouse or partner   1
A friend   2
My son or daughter   3
My brother or sister   4
Some other relative   5
A customer or client   6
Some other person, please specify **[FORCE IF SELECTED]**   7

Q2   **[SHOW IF S8=3]** Was your **[PIPE: S7]** tool gift...?
[SHOW IF S8=1 OR 2] Was your **[PIPE: S7]** tool purchase...?
Please select only one.
[SHOW IF S8=3] An unexpected surprise   1
[SHOW IF S8=3] Something that you specifically requested on your "wish-list"   2
[SHOW IF S8=1 OR 2] An impulse buy   3
[SHOW IF S8=1 OR 2] A planned purchase   4

Q3   In addition to the **[PIPE: S7]** tool you recently acquired, **how many** of the following other brands of tools—if any—do you have in your household?
Please enter those numbers in each of the boxes below.

[RANDOMIZE PRESENTATION ORDER OF LIST ITEMS 1-5]
_1   Sparky
_2   Leatherhead
_3   Trojan Army
_4   London Tower
_5   Crafty
_6   Other, please specify **[FORCE IF SELECTED]**
_7   Other, please specify **[FORCE IF SELECTED]**
_8   No other tools in the household

[DO NOT ALLOW THE CHOICE OF Q3_8 ALONG WITH ANY OTHER Q3 RESPONSES]
[IF Q2=1 *(R's tool was an unsolicited gift)*, **SKIP TO Q6]**
Q4   **[SHOW IF S8=1 OR 2]** Before starting to shop for a tool, which brand(s)—if any— were you considering?

[SHOW IF Q2=2] When you asked for a tool, which specific brand(s)—if any—did you request?

Please select all that apply.
_1   None—I had no specific brands in mind
_2   Sparky
_3   Leatherhead
_4   Trojan Army
_5   London Tower
_6   Crafty
_7   Some other tool brand, please specify **[FORCE IF SELECTED]**

[DO NOT ALLOW THE CHOICE OF Q4_1 ALONG WITH ANY OTHER Q4 RESPONSES]
[IF Q4_1=1 *(R had no specific tool brands in mind)*, SKIP TO Q6]

Q5   **[SHOW S8=1 OR 2]** Did you end up buying one of the brands you originally consid-
        ered before you started shopping?

        [SHOW IF Q2=2] Did you receive the brand you specifically asked for?
        Please select only one.
        Yes   1
        No   2

Q6   **[SHOW S8=1 OR 2]** How much did you pay for the **[PIPE: S7]** tool you purchased?
        [SHOW IF S8=3] If you had to guess, how much do you think your **[PIPE: S7]**
        tool cost? *Please enter your response as a whole number (without decimal points) in
        the space below.*
_   **[ALLOW NUMERIC RESPONSES BETWEEN 1 & 500]**
[IF Q2=1 *(R's tool was an unsolicited gift)*, SKIP TO Q11]

Q7   **[SHOW S8=1 OR 2]** How much research—if any—did you conduct on tools before
        purchasing the **[PIPE: S7]**?
        [SHOW IF S8=3] How much research—if any—did you conduct on tools before put-
        ting it on your "wish list?"

        Please select only one.
        A lot of research   1
        Some research   2
        A little research   3
        No research at all   4

**[IF Q7=4 *(R conducted no tool research prior to purchase)*, SKIP TO Q11] [IF Q7 LE 3, ASK
Q8]**
Q8   Which of the following <u>information sources</u> did you use to research tools?
        Please select all that apply.
        [RANDOMIZE PRESENTATION ORDER OF LIST ITEMS 1–10]
        _1   In-store displays
        _2   Magazines

_3   Catalogs
_4   Hunting/Fishing Guides
_5   Internet/websites
_6   Family or friends
_7   Retail circulars/Newspaper ads
_8   Magazine articles
_9   Television
_10   An employee in a store/salesperson
_11   Some other information source, please specify
_12   Don't know

[DO NOT ALLOW THE CHOICE OF Q8_12 ALONG WITH ANY OTHER Q8 RESPONSES]

> Randomizing lists like these keeps response bias down—some respondents may gravitate toward the first answer—and this at least evens out any such tendency.

Q9   **[SHOW S8=1 OR 2]** Thinking back to your shopping experience, which 3 things did you consider the **most** important in selecting a tool?

        [SHOW IF S8=3] As you were researching tools, which 3 things did you consider the **most** important?

Please rank the top 3 features by entering a "1" next to the most important, a "2" next to the second most important and a "3" for the third most important feature .

        [RANDOMIZE PRESENTATION ORDER OF LIST ITEMS 1–11]

_1   Previous experience with brand
_2   Price
_3   Recommendation from friends or family
_4   Recommendation from a salesperson
_5   Best value for the money
_6   Design
_7   Product packaging
_8   Product display in the store
_9   Read a review or article
_10   Weight
_11   It was on sale
_12   Reputation of the brand
_13   Easy to use
_14   A specific feature or capability of the tool, please specify

> In all likelihood, only the first list would be strictly needed as isolating what is most important would be the objective. Rankings work better than ratings in determining what really matters, as people must choose an order.

Q10   **[SHOW S8=1 OR 2]** Which of the following was **least** important when shopping for tools?

        [SHOW S8=3] Which of the following was **least** important when researching tools?

        Please select only one. **[Present in same order as presented in q9]**

[SHOW IF Q9_1 NE 1, 2 OR 3] Previous experience with brand	1
[SHOW IF Q9_2 NE 1, 2 OR 3] Price	2
[SHOW IF Q9_3 NE 1, 2 OR 3] Recommendation from friends or family	3
[SHOW IF Q9_4 NE 1, 2 OR 3] Recommendation from a salesperson	4
[SHOW IF Q9_5 NE 1, 2 OR 3] Best value for the money	5
[SHOW IF Q9_6 NE 1, 2 OR 3] Design	6
[SHOW IF Q9_7 NE 1, 2 OR 3] Product packaging	7
[SHOW IF Q9_8 NE 1, 2 OR 3] Product display in the store	8
[SHOW IF Q9_9 NE 1, 2 OR 3] Read a review or article	9
[SHOW IF Q9_10 NE 1, 2 OR 3] Weight	10
[SHOW IF Q9_11 NE 1, 2 OR 3] It was on sale	11
[SHOW IF Q9_12 NE 1, 2 OR 3] Reputation of the brand	12
[SHOW IF Q9_13 NE 1, 2 OR 3] Easy to use	13
[SHOW IF Q9_14 NE 1, 2 OR 3] A specific feature or capability	14

Q11A   **[SHOW S8=1 OR 2]** Where did you purchase the **[PIPE: S7]** tool?

        [SHOW IF S8=3] Where was your **[PIPE: S7]** tool purchased—if you know?

Please select only one.
Online/website/retailer
Physical retail store   2
Mail-order catalog   3
Don't know   4

[IF Q11A=2 *(Tool was purchased at a brick-and-mortar store)*, SKIP TO Q11C]
[IF Q11A=3 *(Tool was purchased through a catalog)*, SKIP TO Q11D]
[IF Q11A=4 *(R doesn't know where the tool was purchased)*, SKIP TO Q12]
[IF Q11A=1 *(Tool was purchased online)*, ASK Q11B]

Q11B   **[SHOW S8=1 OR 2]** From which website did you purchase the **[PIPE: S7]** tool?
       [SHOW IF S8=3] From which website was your **[PIPE: S7]** tool purchased—if you
       know?
       Please select only one.
[INSERT ETAILER LIST]

Q11C   **[SHOW S8=1 OR 2]** From which physical retail store did you purchase the **[PIPE: S7]**
       tool?
       [SHOW IF S8=3] From which physical retail store was your **[PIPE: S7]** tool pur-
       chased—if you know?
       Please select only one.
[INSERT PHYSICAL STORE LIST]

Q11D   **[SHOW S8=1 OR 2]** From which catalog did you purchase the **[PIPE: S7]** tool?
       [SHOW IF S8=3] From which catalog was your **[PIPE: S7]** tool purchased—if you
       know?
       Please select only one.
[INSERT CATALOG LIST]

Q12   When—if ever—do you intend to purchase another tool?
       Please select only one.
       By the end of this year   6
       Sometime next year   5
       Sometime the year after   4
       Sometime after that   3
       Not sure   2
       Don't intend to purchase another 1

> Note that the highest frequency is given the highest number code. This will help later if this is used in any form of multivariate analysis, as "more" should have a higher code.

[IF Q12 GE 5 *(R does not intend to purchase another tool or doesn't know)*, SKIP TO Q14]
Q13   Which brand would you **most likely** consider for a future tool purchase?
       Please select only one.
       [RANDOMIZE PRESENTATION ORDER OF LIST ITEMS 1–5]

       Sparky   1
       Leatherhead   2
       Trojan Army   3

London Tower	4
Crafty	5
Some other brand	6
Don't know	7

[IF STATUS=1 OR 3 *(R is a non-tool user or a giver)*, SKIP TO MAX/DIFF EXERCISE]

Product benefits/usage

Q14   Which of the following activities do you use your **[PIPE: S7]** tool for or in conjunction with ? *Please select all that apply.*

[RANDOMIZE PRESENTATION ORDER OF LIST ITEMS 1–12]
- _1   Camping/backpacking
- _2   Cycling
- _3   Boating/sailing
- _4   Fishing
- _5   Gardening
- _6   Hunting
- _7   Vehicle repair
- _8   Arts/crafts
- _9   Home improvement
- _10   Emergency repairs
- _11   Woodworking
- _12   My job
- _13   Some other activity

Q15   Which of the following activities do you use your **[PIPE: S7]** tool for **most** often?
Please select up to 2 activities.

[RANDOMIZE PRESENTATION ORDER OF LIST ITEMS 1–12]
- _1   **[SHOW IF Q14_1=1]**Camping/backpacking
- _2   **[SHOW IF Q14_2=1]**Cycling
- _3   **[SHOW IF Q14_3=1]**Boating/sailing
- _4   **[SHOW IF Q14_4=1]**Fishing
- _5   **[SHOW IF Q14_5=1]**Gardening
- _6   **[SHOW IF Q14_6=1]**Hunting
- _7   **[SHOW IF Q14_7=1]**Vehicle repair
- _8   **[SHOW IF Q14_8=1]**Arts/crafts
- _9   **[SHOW IF Q14_9=1]**Home improvement
- _10   **[SHOW IF Q14_10=1]**Emergency repairs
- _11   **[SHOW IF Q14_11=1]**Woodworking
- _12   **[SHOW IF Q14_12=1]**My job
- _13   **[SHOW IF Q14_13=1] [PIPE Q14_13]**

Q16   Which of the following best describes how you are using your **[PIPE: S7]** tool?

Mostly for activities that I thought I would	1
For activities that I thought **and** for different activities	2
I mostly use my tool for **different** activities than anticipated	3

Max/diff exercise

In a moment we're going to take you through an exercise where you will be asked to evaluate items that you might consider when shopping for a tool. On each screen in this exercise, you will see 3 items. Your task is to review the 3 items and...

✦ Select the **most** important item when shopping for a tool, such as the **[PIPE: S7]** you recently acquired and select the **least** important item when shopping for a tool
The items shown will vary from one screen to another.

Hard attributes	Soft attributes
Quality	Helps me be self-reliant
Durability	Shares my passion
Innovative	Inspires me to be successful
Comfort/grip	Recommended by people I trust
Value	Helps me get the job done
Design	Gives me comfort knowing I have it
Number of tools included	Prepares me for any emergency
Type of tools included	Makes me look cool
Weight	Is something my friends have
Easy to use	I've always wanted one

[SHOW THIS TEXT IMMEDIATELY BEFORE EACH TRADEOFF GRID]
Which of the following items are **most** important and **least** important in selecting a tool?

Brand and brand user imagery profiling

Q17   Which tool brand does each attribute **best** describe?
Please select only one brand for each attribute or "none of these."

Sparky	Leatherhead	Trojan Army	None of these
1	2	3	4

[RANDOMIZE PRESENTATION ORDER OF LIST ITEMS 1–18]

_1   High quality
_2   Durable
_3   Innovative
_4   Best value
_5   User-friendly
_6   Inspires me
_7   Awkward to use
_8   Heavy
_9   Leader
_10   Serious
_11   Ergonomic/ comfortable to use
_12   Versatile
_13   Recommended by people I trust
_14   Fun to use
_15   Trendy
_16   For beginners
_17   Technical
_18   Lightweight

> Note that this exercise asks only for which is best, rather than full ratings for each brand. Knowing which is best is highly important, and can be used in multivariate analyses as ratings would be. This also saves a great deal of time in questioning, important in a long survey.

113

Q18   The following list describes different types of people. What type of person would
      buy these tool brands? *Please select all that apply or none.*

Sparky	Leatherhead	Trojan Army	None of these
1	2	3	4

[RANDOMIZE PRESENTATION ORDER OF LIST ITEMS 1–16]

_1   Would rather do a home remodeling project themselves than hire it out
_2   Spends a lot of time in the garden
_3   Likes to hunt or fish
_4   Takes a lot of adventurous trips
_4   Works in a factory with machinery
_5   Works at a desk in an office
_6   Can fix or repair anything
_7   Can build anything
_8   Is in the military
_9   Loves to watch sports on TV
_10 Is athletic and loves to play sports
_11 Always looks for a bargain
_12 Is a family person
_13 Could survive for weeks in the wilderness
_14 Has tool needs very much like my own
_15 Always has the latest gadgets or tools
_16 Buys the best, regardless of cost

Shopping preferences

Q19   When shopping for gear like tools , where do you most often shop?
      Please select all that apply.
      _1   Online/websites/etailers
      _2   Physical retail stores
      _3   Mail-order catalogs
      _4   Somewhere else
Q20   Which of the following shopping websites would you normally visit to shop for gear
      like a tool?
      Please select all that apply.
[INSERT ETAILER LIST]

Q21   At what retail stores do you normally shop for gear like tools?
      Please select all that apply.
[INSERT PHYSICAL STORE LIST]

Q22   Which catalogs do you normally shop for gear like tools?
      Please select all that apply.
[INSERT CATALOG LIST]

114

Self perception profiling

Q23   Now, we will present a series of statements that may or may not describe a person like yourself. For each statement, please tell us how much you agree or disagree that the statement describes **you**. *For each statement listed below, select the answer that comes closest to how well it describes you.*

[DO NOT SHOW NUMERIC SCALE VALUES]

Disagree strongly	Disagree somewhat	Disagree slightly	Agree slightly	Agree somewhat	Agree strongly
1	2	3	4	5	6

  _1   I prefer to fix things myself whenever possible
  _2   I am typically the best prepared person I know for an emergency
  _3   People often ask me for advice
  _4   I like to plan for all possibilities
  _5   I organize activities for my group of friends
  _6   Friends and family bring me things to repair
  _7   It is wise to have a tool always available
  _8   I take a tool everywhere I go
  _9   It typically is more sensible to carry a tool than a knife

Q24   Which of the following activities do you participate in <u>regularly</u> ?

Please select all that apply.
  _1   Automotive work
  _2   Bible/devotional
  _3   Boating/sailing
  _4   Camping/hiking
  _5   Casino gambling
  _6   Charitable giving
  _7   Crafts
  _8   Cultural arts/events
  _9   Cycling
  _10   Do-it-yourself projects
  _11   Fishing
  _12   Fitness/exercise
  _13   Gardening
  _14   Golf
  _15   Gourmet cooking/food/wines
  _16   Grandchildren
  _17   Home decorating
  _18   Hunting/shooting
  _19   Investments (stocks, mutual funds)
  _20   Movie watching
  _21   Personal computing/Internet
  _22   Pets: Cats
  _23   Pets: Dogs
  _24   Photography
  _25   Read books

_26   Self-improvement
_27   Snow skiing
_28   Soccer
_29   Sweepstakes/contests
_30   Tennis
_31   Travel – Domestic
_32   Travel – Foreign
_33   TV shopping
_34   Vitamins/natural foods
_35   Watching TV

Media habits

Q25   In a typical week, how many hours do you spend doing the following activities?
Please enter a number for each activity below. Zero is an acceptable response.
[RANDOMIZE PRESENTATION ORDER OF LIST ITEMS 1–4]
_1   Reading the newspaper
_2   Reading magazines
_3   Watching television
_4   Surfing the internet (excluding email)

[IF Q25_1=0, SKIP TO PROGRAMMER INSTRUCTIONS THAT FOLLOW Q26]
[IF Q25_1 GE 1, ASK Q26]

Q26   Which of the following newspapers do you read on a regular basis?
Please select all that apply.
_1   Local or regional newspaper
_2   Los Angeles Times
_3   New York Times
_4   USA Today
_5   Wall Street Journal
_6   Washington Post
_7   Some other newspaper, please specify **[FORCE IF SELECTED]**

[IF Q25_2=0, SKIP TO PROGRAMMER INSTRUCTIONS THAT FOLLOW Q27]
Q27   Which of the following magazines do you read on a regular basis?
Please select all that apply.
_1   AARP
_2   Better Homes & Gardens
_3   Car and Driver
_4   ESPN the Magazine
_5   Field & Stream
_6   Golf Digest
_7   Golf Magazine
_8   Maxim
_9   Men's Health
_10   Money
_11   National Geographic
_12   Newsweek

> Detailed information about media habits in places where the client could advertise will help reach target groups selectively, especially when incorporated into a gains analysis (as discussed on pages 85 to 87.

_13	People
_14	Playboy
_15	Popular Science
_16	Reader's Digest
_17	Real Simple
_18	Sports Illustrated
_19	Stuff
_20	Sunset
_21	TIME
_22	TV Guide
_23	U.S. News & World Report
_24	Some other magazine, please specify **[FORCE IF SELECTED]**

[IF Q25_3=0, SKIP TO PROGRAMMER INSTRUCTIONS THAT FOLLOW Q29]
[IF Q25_3 GE 1, ASK Q28]

Q28   Which <u>type</u> of television programs do you regularly watch?
Please select all that apply.

_1	Action/Adventure
_2	Cartoon
_3	Childrens
_4	Comedy
_5	Drama
_6	Game Show
_7	News
_8	Reality
_9	Science Fiction
_10	Soap Operas
_11	Sports
_12	Talk Shows
_13	Some other type of show, please specify **[FORCE IF SELECTED]**

Q29   Which of the <u>following</u> TV shows do you regularly watch?
Please select all that apply.

_1	48 Hours
_2	60 Minutes
_3	America's Got Talent
_4	Big Brother
_5	Cold Case
_6	Criminal Minds
_7	CSI: Crime Scene Investigation
_8	Hell's Kitchen
_9	House
_10	How I Met Your Mother
_11	Last Comic Standing
_12	Law & Order
_13	Rock Star
_14	So You Think You Can Dance
_15	Two and a Half Men
_16	Without a Trace
_17	Some other TV show, please specify

Q30   Which of the following <u>websites</u> do you regularly visit?

Please select all that apply.

_1   amazon.com
_2   aol.com
_3   bestbuy.com
_4   circuitcity.com
_5   cnn.com
_6   comcast.net
_7   drudgereport.com
_8   ebay.com
_9   foxnews.com
_10   foxsports.com
_11   geocities.com
_12   google.com
_13   hotmail.com
_14   imdb.com
_15   mapquest.com
_16   microsoft.com
_17   msn.com
_18   myspace.com
_19   neopets.com
_20   nytimes.com
_21   paypal.com
_22   slashdot.org
_23   symantec.com
_24   weather.com
_25   wellsfargo.com
_26   wikipedia.org
_27   xanga.com
_28   yahoo.com
_29   Some other website

Demographics

D1   Just a few final questions for classification purposes. Again, all your answers are strictly confidential and will be used only in combination with the answers of others.

Are you...?
Male   1
Female   2

D2   What is the highest level of education you've completed?
Please select only one.
High school or less   1
Technical/trade diploma/certificate   2
Some college or university   3
University degree/under-graduate degree   4
Graduate degree/ Master's degree   5
Post-graduate degree/doctorate   6

D3   Including you, how many adults (age 18 and over) live in your household?

Please enter your answer below. If you live in more than one household, please answer for the household in which you spend most of your time.

    _1   Number of adults in household: **[ANSWER BOX: ALLOW NUMERIC RESPONSES BETWEEN 1 & 50]**
    _2   Prefer not to answer **[CHECK BOX]**

D4   How many children under the age of 18 live in your household?

Please enter your answer below. If you live in more than one household, please answer for the same household you had in mind when answering the previous question.

    _1   Number of children in household: **[ANSWER BOX: ALLOW NU-MERIC RESPONSES BETWEEN 0 & 15]**
    _2   Prefer not to answer **[CHECK BOX]**

D5   How would you describe your primary residence?

    _1   Single family (detached) home
    _2   Multi-family (connected) home

    _3   Owned
    _4   Rented

    _5   Prefer not to answer **[CHECK BOX]**

[DO NOT ALLOW THE CHOICE OF D5_5 ALONG WITH ANY OTHER D5 RESPONSES]

D6   Please enter your 5-digit ZIP code in the space below?

Please enter 5 digits in the space below.

    _1   Zip code: **[ANSWER BOX: ALLOW NUMERIC RESPONSES BETWEEN 11111 & 99999]**
    _2   Prefer not to answer **[CHECK BOX]**

D7   What is your race or ethnicity?

Please select only one.
White/Caucasian   1
African American   2
Asian/Pacific Islander   3
Hispanic/Latino   4
Some other race or ethnicity   5
Prefer not to answer **[CHECK BOX]**   6

D8   What was your household's approximate total income last year before taxes? Was it...?

Please select only one.

Less than $50,000	1
At least $50,000 but less than $75,000	2
At least $75,000 but less than $100,000	3
At least $100,000 but less than $150,000	4
At least $150,000 but less than $200,000	5
$200,000 or more	6
Prefer not to answer	7

D9   Finally, in the past 2 weeks, have you answered the exact same set of questions you an-
        swered just now in any other web or phone survey?

Please select only one.

I definitely have	1
I might have, but I'm not sure	2
I definitely have not	3

[TOP 100 TV SHOWS LIST]
24
30 Days
7th Heaven
Alias
American Idol
America's Next Top Model
Angel
Avatar: The Last Airbender
Battlestar Galactica (2003)
Beverly Hills, 90210
Big Brother
Blade
Bleach
Bones
Boy Meets World
Buffy the Vampire Slayer
Charmed
Criminal Minds
CSI
CSI: Miami
CSI: NY
Dancing With the Stars
Danny Phantom
Days of our Lives
[THIS LIST GOES ON FROM HERE]

[ETAILER LIST]	[PHYSICAL STORE LIST]	[CATALOG LIST]
aafes.com	Ace Hardware	Bass Pro Shops
amazon.com	Academy Sports & Outdoors	Cabela's
backcountry.com	Army & Air Force Exchange	Campmor
basspro.com	Bass Pro Shops	Grainger
brookstone.com	Big 5 Sporting Goods	Herrington
buy.com	Brookstone	Improvements
cabelas.com	Cabela's	JCPenney
campingworld.com	Campmor	L.L. Bean
campmor.com	Copeland Sports	Orvis
costco.com	Costco	REI
dickssportinggoods.com	Dick's Sporting Goods	Sears
ebay.com	Eastern Mountain Sports	Sierra Outdoors
eddiebauer.com	G.I. Joe's	Skymall
ems.com)	Grainger	Sportsman's Guide
fogdog.com	Home Depot	Some other catalog
geardirect.com	JCPenney	Don't know
gijoes.com	K-mart	
grainger.com	L.L. Bean	
homedepot.com	Lowes	
jcpenney.com	REI	
kmart.com	Sears	
llbean.com	Sport Chalet	
lowes.com	Sports Authority	
paragonsports.com	Wal-mart	
qvc.com	Some other physical retail store	
rei.com	Don't know	
sears.com		
shop.com		
sportsauthority.com		
target.com		
walmart.com		

Thank you for your interest in this study. However, we have already reached our goal for the number of completed surveys by individuals with your background. We appreciate your willingness to share your opinions with us and hope that you'll participate in future surveys.

[BUTTON TEXT: *Click here to close browser window***] [ACTION:** *Close the browser window***]**

[SURVEY CLOSED SCREEN]

Thank you for your interest in this study; however, we have already achieved our goal for the number of responses required. We appreciate your willingness to share your opinions with us and hope you'll participate in future surveys.

[BUTTON TEXT: *Click here to close browser window***] [ACTION:** *Close the browser window***]**

[CLOSING SCREEN]

Those are all of the questions we have for you today. Your responses have been recorded, and your participation in this survey is now complete. Thank you for your time.

Please enter the email address to which you'd like us to send your gift certificate.

Email address:

You can expect to receive your gift certificate at this email address by **[DATE]**.

[BUTTON TEXT: *Click here to close browser window***] [ACTION:** *Close the browser window***]**

> As in any survey, you need to have a means to ease out people who do not qualify. Expect some calls in any event, as some people will be sure that they should take the survey even if your quota for that group has long been filled. Some people may even sign on multiple times after being politely turned away and then complain about that also.

Appendix

Data Types: Definitions

Some types of variables (question items) convey more numerical information than others. Some confusion can arise about the numerical information that variables contains, and differences between the types of variables.

This lack of clarity may come in part from references made to **data scales**. The term **scale** brings to mind such devices as measuring cups and yardsticks. However, the information in marketing research scales often has less numerical information than yardstick-type scales, and cannot be manipulated in the same ways. We would not, as an extreme example, supply number codes to respondents' home towns, and then average these to determine which town is "typical."

Here are the basic types of data.

Nominal data contains the least numerical information of the data types. A nominal-level variable could be, for example, the region in which the respondent lives. In analyzing the data, you would assign the regions codes, perhaps like this:

Northwest = 1   Midwest = 2   South = 3   West = 4.

The codes have no real numeric value (that is, a code 3 is not "worth" more than code 1, for instance). The codes simply hold the place of the names. No set distance exists between the codes, nor is there any numerical order to the codes.

Ordinal data. The codes here show an order or ranking, but not the distance between the rankings. For instance, you might ask respondents to rank 10 cities, based on how much they would like to live in each, overall. Using this type of scale, you could not say that the respondent likes the first city on the list 10 times more than the last. Nor could you say that the gap between cities 1 and 2 on the list is the same size as the gap between cities 2 and 3, or between any other pair of cities separated by one ranking.

Ordinal data or rankings among a group of people can be converted to **ratio-level data** by a process called Thurstone's Case 5. This has been in use in psychometrics since about 1930, and so it has a long track record. As mentioned, the procedure works at the group level as it is commonly done—it is a comparison of the rankings by all the people in a group that leads to the rescaling. This is often linked with a partial sorting method called Q-Sort . Together these methods have been used to provide interval level data for up to 100 items being compared. Even if comparisons are for a group, no other method can clearly provide a hierarchy for quite so many items.

Interval scales. These contain a constant unit of measurement, and so allow statements about the differences between the scales. However, the zero point selected on these scales is arbitrary. Temperature on the Fahrenheit or Celsius scales would be an example of an interval measure. It is not correct to say that a temperature of 80° F is "twice as hot" as 40° F. However, you can certainly say that the first temperature is 40 degrees higher than the second.

Ratio scales. These contain the most arithmetic information, and can be subjected to the most manipulation of all scale types. Distance in feet is one example of a ratio measure. Obviously, we can say that four feet is twice as far as two feet, as we can say that the second measure is two feet more than the first.

Differences in types of data scales matter because many statistical procedures, including most multivariate ones, will not work with nominal-level data. There has been some debate over many years about using ordinal data with many forms of analysis. In general, either interval-level data or ratio-level data will work with nearly all multivariate procedures.

The term **metric data** can be used to describe both interval-level and ordinal-level data, since they both use a set scale with even intervals.

Non-metric data would then include both ordinal-level and nominal-level data.

Dependent and Independent

Some confusion may also arise about the use of the terms **dependent** and **independent variables**. Not all procedures make this distinction, and different terms may get used.

Clustering procedures, for instance, do not typically have any dependent or independent variables. Instead, we refer to basis (or grouping) variables and descriptor variables. Factor analysis also does not make use of a dependent variable, but rather seeks to combine variables into broad underlying "themes" or factors.

In procedures using a **dependent** variable, that variable is actually the crux of the analysis. The other variables in the study (the **independent** variables) explain or predict patterns in the dependent. In a regression, for instance, the dependent variable gets described by an equation manipulating the other variables.

In discriminant analysis, the dependent variable often is called the **grouping variable**. This variable shows each respondent's membership in some group. The other variables are then generate functions that most strongly differentiate between the groups.

Many different variables can be used to group respondents in this type of analysis. For instance, suppose you had respondents rate a product from 1 to 5 on an overall scale. Those who rated the product "5" overall could become one group, those rating it "4" another group, and so on. You could then run discriminant analysis on these 5 groups, to see what most differentiates those who gave the product a high rating form those who gave it a low rating.

CHAID (Chi-squared AID) and CRT and related methods use a **dependent grouping variable**, like discriminant analysis. However, CHAID divides and re-divides the sample to best differentiate between the groups represented in the dependent variable. CHAID will generate segments in a way that most strongly differentiates between the groups analyzed—but only at each location where there is a split. CHAID's splitting of a sample leads to a tree-like division plan. Groups at the end of a given branch will differ significantly. Going from one branch of the tree to another, you may encounter groups with similar incidences of the various segments.

Principal References

Aldenderfer, M. S. & Blashfield, R. K. (1988). Cluster Analysis. (Sage: Newbury Park, CA.).

Bagozzi, R (1994) Advanced Marketing Research. (Cambridge, MA. Blackwell Publishers)

Everitt, B. (1982). Cluster Analysis. (2nd Ed.) (New York: Halsted).

Green, P. E., Tull, D. S. & Albaum, G. (1978). Research for Marketing Decisions. (Englewood Cliffs, N.J.: Prentice-Hall).

Haley, R.I. (1968). "Benefit Segmentation: a Decision Oriented Research Tool", Journal of Marketing, 32.

Hagenaars, J. A. and McCutcheon, A. L. (eds.) (2002). Applied Latent Class Analysis. (Cambridge: Cambridge University Press).

James, M. (1985). Classification Algorithms. (London: Wiley).

Jedidi,K, Harsharanjeet J. S., and DeSarbo W. (1997). "Finite-Mixture Structural Equation Models for Response-Based Segmentation and Unobserved Heterogeneity." Marketing Science, 16, 1

Kass, G. (1980). An exploratory technique for investigating large quantities of categorical data. Applied Statistics, 29

Kaufmann, L. & Rousseeuw, P.J. (1990). Finding Groups in Data. (New York: John Wiley and Sons).

Luke, D. (2004). Multilevel Modeling (Quantitative Applications in the Social Sciences). (Thousand Oaks, CA: Sage Publications).

McDonald, M. and Dunbar, I. (2005). Market Segmentation (Butterworth Heinemann: Oxford).

Myers, J. H. & Tauber, E. (1977). Market Structure Analysis. (Chicago: American Marketing Association).

Neal, W. D. (1989). "A Comparison of 18 Clustering Algorithms Generally Available to the Marketing Research Professional." Sawtooth Software Conference Proceedings.

Punji, G. and Stewart, D. R. (1983). "Cluster Analysis in Marketing Research: Review and Suggestions for Application." Journal of Marketing Research, XX (May).

Schaffer, C. M & Green, P.E. (1996). "An Empirical Comparison of Variable Standardization Methods in Cluster Analysis." Multivariate Behavior Research 31 (2).

Schaffer, C. M. & Green, P.E. (1998). "Cluster-based Market Segmentation: Some Further Comparisons of Alternative Approaches." Journal of the Market Research Society, 40 (2) (April).

Smith, W. R. (1956). "Product Differentiation and Market Segmentation as Alternative Marketing Strategies." Journal of Marketing (July).

Sonquist, J. A., & Dunkelburg, W. C. (1977). <u>Survey and Opinion Research.</u> (Englewood Cliffs, New Jersey: Prentice-Hall).

Stewart, D. W. (1981). " The Application and Misapplication of Factor Analysis in Marketing Research." <u>Journal of Marketing Research,</u> XVIII, (February).

Struhl, S (1992). Some Specialized Problem-solving Applications of CHAID. <u>Quirk's Marketing Research Review</u> VI (9) (Quirk's Review: Minneapolis, MN).

Sundberg, Rolf (1976). "An iterative method for solution of the likelihood equations for incomplete data from exponential families." <u>Communications in Statistics – Simulation and Computation</u> 5 (1).

Thurstone, L.L. (1927). A Law of Comparative Judgment. <u>Psychological Review,</u> 34, 278-286.

Thurstone, L.L. (1929). The Measurement of Psychological Value. In T.V. Smith and W.K. Wright (Eds.), <u>Essays in Philosophy by Seventeen Doctors of Philosophy of the University of Chicago.</u> Chicago: Open Court.

Tull, D. S. and Hawkins, D. I. (1980). <u>Marketing Research.</u> (2nd ed.). (Englewood Cliffs, N.J.: Macmillan).

Wilkie, W. L. (1971). "Market Segmentation Research: A Conceptual Analysis," Paper No. 324, Institute for Research in the Behavioral, Economic and Management Sciences. (Purdue University).

Wind, Y. (1978). "Issues and Advances in Segmentation Research." <u>Journal of Marketing Research,</u> XV, (August).

Wind, Y. and Claycamp, H. (1976). "Planning Product Line Strategy: A Matrix Approach." <u>Journal of Marketing,</u> 40 (January).

Wu, C. F. Jeff (1983). "On the Convergence Properties of the EM Algorithm." <u>Annals of Statistics,</u> 11 (1) (March).

Young, Ott and Feigin (1978). "Some Practical Considerations in Market Research," <u>Journal of Marketing Research</u> 15 (3) (August).

Web citations

SPSS TwoStep cluster

http://www.spss.ch/upload/1122644952_The%20SPSS%20TwoStep%20Cluster%20Component.pdf

SPAD software:

http://www.the-data-mine.com/Software/SPAD

Utilities in DCM and conjoint

http://www.sawtoothsoftware.com/forum.php?cmd=show&thread=260&posts=4.

The author dictating for posterity.

End

24426052R00077

Made in the USA
Middletown, DE
23 September 2015